The Daily Breath

Also by Scott A. Morofsky
Wellativity:
In-Powering Wellness Through Communication

The Daily Breath

Transform Your Life One Breath at a Time

SCOTT A. MOROFSKY

Cover design by Laura Hagerty
Cover photo copyright © 2014 Laura Hagerty

Published by Wellativity, LLC
First Edition
ISBN-13: 978-0692258002
ISBN-10: 0692258000

Printed in the United States of America

For Laura Hagerty

From its very inception she worked unceasingly toward the success of The Daily Breath. For weathering the ups and downs as we finalized the content, for her professional editing and formatting, and for her beautiful cover photography she deserves the highest praise.
Thank you, Laura!

So Breathe It.

Preface

The Daily Breath was originally a live stress-management phone service, created by me in the early to mid-1980s. During several successful years, I became proficient in managing the many different features that made up the calls. Each individual call became a valid application to the individual client's life through being tailored to his or her individual needs, using breathing reminders and exercises, personalized affirmations, visualizations, spiritual/metaphysical rhetoric, and goal-oriented reinforcements. All of these techniques were derived from my own schooling, therapeutic training, and personal quest for health, well-being, and spirituality.

Although many valuable daily reader books are available, *Wellativity's The Daily Breath* is unique. As you read the messages, your breathing habits will improve, and you will notice the connections made with breathing in countless life situations.

Having been personally and professionally involved in spiritual, therapeutic, health, fitness, and recovery modalities for almost 30 years, I've incorporated a *practical application* of breathing conditioning in all of the above genres. I refer to many everyday situations and environments in the messages. They include health clubs, food, shopping, driving, exercise, codependency, substance abuse, relationships, family, work-related situations, safety, personal loss, handling success/failure, preventing injury, and many more. If you read The Daily Breath on a daily, weekly, or any other regular basis and you find yourself in similar aforementioned situations, it is certain that you will let your breathing conditioning effortlessly work toward healthier and more inner-connected living.

You will notice that my preferred term for our life source is "God." However, I often use such other terms as Higher Power, Universal Life, Life Energy, etc. No matter what your religious or spiritual inclinations are, or are not, I strongly urge you not to let my choice of terms turn you away from the essence of using your conscious breathing as a means of connecting to your source of life, *as you understand it.*

What you have before you offers many ways to improve the quality of your breathing. The first step is, of course, to begin reading The Daily Breath, once a day or as many as you'd like in one sitting. Whether you are aware of it or not, the quality of your respiration will be improving not only with each conscious breath you take but also with each time you read the words *breathe, inhale, exhale, breathing, breath,* and *So Breathe It.* Moreover, you'll notice this filtering out into your life. For example, when you see or hear these words, you will naturally take fuller breaths more and more often. This means higher levels of oxygen throughout your body, which ultimately translates into healthier and stronger functions on all levels.

On mental, emotional, and spiritual levels the readings are much like other inspirational writings. When we read passages that we identify as truth, we are uplifted in countless ways. This dimension of The Daily Breath is what Wellativity calls "being In-Powered." In addition, you'll notice Wellativity's 12 Principles listed just after this preface. They are derived from the original 12-step programs with the intention of translating them into workable and contemporary language for people with what I call "cross-over afflictions." It's meant to address procrastination, lethargy, sabotage, defiance, and other behaviors that everybody (not just a hardcore addict) experiences. Acknowledging, working with, and letting go of some of our unhealthier behaviors that the 12 Principles help to address in turn brings us back to easier and healthier breathing.

So Breathe It.

You will be able to follow up The Daily Breath readings at **www.wellativity.com**. We offer an ever-increasing supply of Audio Daily Breaths as well as personalized messages and services for just about every aspect of health, healing, well-being, recovery, and fitness.

The Twelve Principles

Principle One

We declared that we needed help healing our bodies, that our health and fitness were becoming very difficult to manage.

Principle Two

Came to understand that God's support would guide us back to good health and the joy of movement.

Principle Three

Made a choice to allow God's power within to help us live healthy lives.

Principle Four

Looked deeply and honestly as we took stock of our physical conditions.

Principle Five

Told the truth to God, ourselves, and another person whom we trusted, the exact conditions of our health and fitness.

Principle Six

Became completely ready and willing to have the source of life within work with us toward healing our minds and bodies.

Principle Seven

With a sense of humility, asked our Higher Power to help restore us to a place of health and vitality.

Principle Eight

Made a list of all the destruction we had contributed to our bodies and our lives. Then became willing to compassionately take restorative actions to all involved, except when to do so would be harmful or unacceptable to ourselves or others.

Principle Nine

Took direct action in healing our bodies wherever it felt right, making sure to keep safety as a priority.

Principle Ten

Continued to question what was working or not, and when adjustments were needed, made them as nonjudgmentally as possible.

Principle Eleven

Sought through appropriate physical and spiritual practices to stay consciously connected to our source of life within, asking ourselves to remain completely open to its guidance and to focus on our willingness to act from a loving place rather than from fear.

Principle Twelve

Having had a deep transformation as a result of these principles, we live by example and unconditionally practice these truths to the best of our abilities throughout our lives.

The Daily Breath

Note: As with all physical exercise, if you have any medical conditions, it's recommended that you check with a qualified health professional first before engaging in any of the suggested exercises described throughout The Daily Breath.

January 1
BREATHING FITNESS

Most people will know what is meant by lung capacity. What is not common knowledge is how to increase it. The first thing to understand is that the act of breathing is done primarily by the diaphragm muscle. It resides just below the lungs and on top of the liver and stomach (and the other surrounding organs). Exercise, singing, shouting, and coughing all work the diaphragm.

Here is one of several breathing exercises that will stretch and strengthen this critical muscle:
1. Breathe in as deeply as you can without causing discomfort.
2. Hold your breath for 3 to 5 seconds.
3. Gently, without forcing or pushing, allow yourself to begin to exhale completely.
4. Once most of the air is out of your lungs, then intentionally and gently push the rest out (this should take about 3 seconds).
5. Then let your breathing return to normal.

Try this several times over the next few days and see if it works for you to practice this technique on a regular basis. Improving our breathing fitness is related to physical fitness. Healthier muscles burn fat and calories more efficiently at a resting heart rate. This is relative to breathing in that a healthier diaphragm, lung capacity, and flexibility of the surrounding muscles make breathing more efficient while resting. This helps keep oxygen levels elevated at all times.

So Breathe It.

1

January 2
TRIGGERING BREATH

From a purely physiological aspect, breathing is triggered by the amount of carbon dioxide in the lungs and/or blood. People acquire breathing habits by many influences. The Daily Breath attempts to change our breathing patterns by outside reminders. By reading these pages you are consciously and subconsciously building healthier habits.

As *Wellativity's Daily Breath* has indicated in other readings, it can't be overemphasized to choose or make some personalized reminders for you to breathe and put them in a variety of places. Writing a message on a sticky note or on your computer, or choosing a color or sound to remind you to breathe at different times and places, is wise. A refrigerator, a desk, a screen saver, etc., are just some of the endless places you can place a reminder to breathe. Draw upon your innate creative birthrights to improve your most basic physical necessity. We all learned unconsciously how to limit our breathing cycles. Now it's your choice to consciously change them to improve the quality of the rest of your life.

The chakra or energy center responsible for breathing has a color. It is commonly seen as blue. If we all let the color blue trigger us to full healthy breathing, our well-being would improve drastically.

So Breathe It.

January 3
AFFIRMING HIS PRESENCE

When we start a prayer, where are we coming from? Why are we praying? Are we trying to get or change something? These questions are not to judge our needs and desires in communicating with God or our Higher Power. Rather, I've found them helpful in clearing my thoughts and feelings upon entering an inner Holy Communion, or prayer.

I often find that when I initially speak a prayer, even the tone of my voice can indicate a distance between myself and my one true parent and source of life. Here is a simple exercise: close your eyes, take a breath, and say "God." Do your best to say "God" as if you were affirming His presence. Notice your feelings when you speak His name, or whatever you might call Him/Her/It. When you do this it can help tremendously in prayer conditioning. Don't forget to breathe; He will wait.

Hello, God. In the highest respect, I acknowledge that You are with me in all Your glory, right now, and forevermore. I'm saying this in my prayer to open the door to Your holy presence for my thinking, more than as a supplication to You. Thank You for always being closer than I can ever imagine. Amen.

So Breathe It.

January 4
GIVE US OUR DAILY BREATH

Let me set out on this day as I focus on my breath of life.

Thank You, God, let each breath stand as an unspoken THANK-YOU.

During this day I pray that our Wills shall be One.

When I forget this original intent, I thank You in advance for the help You freely send me to recall.

When I remember You are carrying me through difficulties, I breathe easier.

The more I choose to think of You, my true father, I feel the hope and glory I know You wish for me.

Knowing You are the essence of love and forgiveness, I choose to stay in that energy.

In my every breath I thank You, God. Amen.

So Breathe It.

January 5
THE HOLDING JOURNAL

Journaling can be one of the most valuable tools toward learning what works and what doesn't in our lives. Many behaviors in my life that can use healthy adjustments usually have patterns, or times and places in which they occur. Being aware of these patterns and keeping a record of them will assist in eliminating them. Changing behaviors so often takes many, many times of just noticing them before we are ready, willing, and able to expedite improvements.

I recommend we all keep a "breathing journal." More precisely, it would be a journal for when we notice we are holding our breaths. To start it now doesn't necessarily mean putting it in written form, even though that would prove to be beneficial. For me today, I've been aware that I have held my breath during (1) washing dishes; (2) showering; (3) bending to tie my shoes; (4) even writing this Daily Breath. Just start with one time you're aware that you are holding your breath. Beginning your "holding journal" now, I promise, will provide unending benefits.

As one of most truthful statement declares: To be aware is to be alive. No better does this journaling pertain to our number one lifeline, breathing.

So Breathe It.

January 6
CONNECTION WITHIN

Whether it is prayer, meditation, chanting, or affirmations, does it not always come down to the same thing? What works best for each of us with regard to consciously connecting with our Higher Power or with the God of our understanding. The intent of the Daily Breath messages is preparation and conditioning. When we are reminded to breathe, it's the first step in preparing us to shift our perception, as well as an immediate tension reducer. In the end it's all really meant to deepen our connection with the reality of life within our being. This inner connection is one of the few things with which we have true control and power. The tool of our breathing is a manual connector to all that resides within. Stop breathing for long enough, and the game of life as we know it ends. I say this not to upset you but just to emphasis the privilege of choosing to connect through our breathing.

Thank You, God, for the freedom to choose. This I understand is the way You designed us.

So Breathe It.

January 7
OXYGENATION

Let's be clear on the immense value of undergoing this program of breathing exercises. If at the very least you have managed one or two additional full breaths, you will have accomplished something. It might help to be well informed about some of the benefits in improving our breathing patterns.

There is a medical belief that by fully oxygenating our cells (this is known as ozone therapy) we create a cellular environment that makes it very difficult for cancer cells to exist.

In addition, there's also a medical belief that by consistently and abundantly filling our cells with oxygen we in all probability are fighting the onset of age-related mental dysfunctions such as Alzheimer's and several other diseases that seem to flourish in an oxygen-deprived environment. When we exercise we increase our breathing and thus increase our oxygen intake.

Isn't this enough inspirational information to convince you that by working with your breathing on a regular basis, you can contribute to your health and well-being?

Breathing Works!

So Breathe It.

January 8
LETTING THE PAST GO

I recently found out that someone from my childhood holds resentment toward me. Being a man committed to the healing not only of myself but of humanity, one of the most difficult things for me to deal with is being powerless with regard to another's healing. One of my favorite affirmations (which applies to this person from my past) is: I do my best and leave the rest.

To align this affirmation with my breathing during prayer and meditation, on my inhale I say, "I do my best," and on the exhale I say, "and leave the rest." This can be done with most affirmative phrases. I also breathe in and whisper, "Be still and know," and then I breathe out and whisper, "That I am one with God."

I affirm, "God grants me the serenity to accept the things I cannot change, the courage to change the things I can, and the wisdom to know the difference."

So Breathe It.

January 9
IN THE PROCESS OF LIFE ITSELF

I was recently sitting in a movie theatre watching an emotional film that seemed to tap the core parental issues of most of the viewers. I say this due to the conversation after the movie. My friend and I were in tears, as were so many of the others, some actually sobbing. I mention this because we both agreed that in the release of this deep sadness, even though outwardly it was because of what was being watched, we in turn identified with our feelings. By sharing them with each other, we were able to experience a degree of our own healing.

Those of us who are on an acknowledged spiritual path in life know how important healing of the mind, body, and spirit is. We've all had our moments of questioning whether we are indeed healing. The message here is that we can breathe easier just by knowing that our Higher Power puts us in situations that will instigate healing, just in the process of life itself.

Let's affirm all is in Divine order. No matter what, our lives serve His higher purpose. He created us, He knows how to fix us! Trust the process.

So Breathe It.

January 10
SHHHH . . .

Sometimes when my mother wanted to help me relax, she would quietly say, "Shhhh, everything is OK, I'm here." To this day still, when I close my eyes and exhale a long, soft "shhhh," I can experience a profound release of tension. Another comforting thing she would do was to gently run her fingers through my hair. When I do this myself, I can immediately find a more peaceful place to rejuvenate. Is there some action that brings you to a more centered or grounded place? Maybe it's a phrase of a song someone sang to or around you that brings you to a pleasant place. This is the essence of stress reduction. Closing our eyes, having a peaceful thought, and taking a few relaxed breaths can do the trick when it comes to reconnecting within.

Let there be Peace on Earth and let it begin with my breathing.

So Breathe It.

January 11
RELAXED FOCUS

People will come to read these words for many reasons. No matter what your reason is, I hope you'll put this book down with a deeper experience of peace, clarity, and joy. I heard once that bliss is the space between our thoughts. I've found the best way to get in-between my thoughts is to focus on something that requires little or no thought. A candle's flame, a mandala, the ocean, or just a relaxed focus on my breathing can help me to just "be" for what I see as a precious or sacred segment of time. The endless stream of thoughts, as always, will be there when I choose to bring my focus back to them. Every moment we commune with our Power Within, it's as if we are recharging our batteries or energy cells. By having this relaxed focus on the Source of Life, we absorb its Energy simply by facing it.

Thank You, God, for the freedom to choose where and what to focus on. Amen.

So Breathe It.

January 12
GRATITUDE FOR ALL

Gratitude for all can be quite a challenge. We might have an ever-increasing list of things we're grateful to have; even some we're grateful not to have. But when we say "for all," that means for EVERYTHING and EVERYBODY in our lives. Oh boy, now it can get difficult. Even for the boss I despise? Even for my disability? YES! Without exception, once I've gotten past my initial thoughts and feelings about the things that most challenge me, I have always been able to extract some value toward how these apparent negatives have contributed to my overall growth.

This concept, if harnessed, can bring us to a place of gratitude, 24/7. Here's a thought I use in the most trying situations: "Oh God, right now I really don't like or appreciate this. God, I'm taking a whole lot of breaths in order to not act impulsively toward my negative perception. God, please lift my smaller vision of what I want, so that I may open to what is best for me. I know when I let go of the cloud of my selfishness, we'll once again commune in the light of infinite thankfulness. Amen."

When Christ said "make friends with your enemies," could it be possible that He also meant us to be grateful for the lessons and opportunities even they bring to you?

So Breathe It.

January 13
WALKING WITH WATER

Recently I was carrying a large, full, open container of water. At one point or another most of us have had this experience of attempting not to spill any of the swaying water as we slowly walked. As I was carefully walking, I was intrigued with what it took to manage my body, the container, and the water. It became clear that by looking at the center of the water below and gently breathing while I pictured the way a cat would move with its stealth, I spilled not a drop of water.

The next time we are challenged by a situation that presents us with the chance of losing our focus, center, or overall balance, why don't we do our best to carry the situation (or open container of water) by gently breathing as we turn our actions and thoughts over to the Power Within us? If we give it the opportunity, the Power Within will run the event far better than we could by going it alone.

Each step, breath, thought—please, God, take them from me and transform me from within. I open the door to my soul for Your entrance. Thank You. Amen.

So Breathe It.

January 14
SPIRITUAL ARMOR

I once heard someone use the term *spiritual armor.* At first I related to the physical type of armor, commonly made of metal. Then I wondered what qualities would be needed for something or someone to be armored by spirit.

Certainly my Higher Power, guardian angels, and/or God must be on my side for me to be protected in that fashion. I also came to the conclusion that I would have to do what was needed for complete safety to be rendered. In my opinion, my part is humbly asking and having complete faith in knowing my safekeeping is, and will continue to be. Didn't an infinitely wise prophet once say that in order to multiply what we are in need of we must give thanks for it already being so?

From this spot until the next spot in which I pray and breathe, I thank You, God, for my safekeeping.

So Breathe It.

January 15
BLOWN AWAY

Somewhere along the path of my spiritual journey I learned a meditation technique that made a significant difference in how I dealt with quiet times within myself. When my thoughts seem to be intense, stressful, and immovable, I imagine my mind as a room. In that room are two open windows on opposite walls. In each breath, I feel a breeze coming in one window as it passes through my mental room. Each stressful thought is ushered out the opposite window with every exhale.

This method is more effective at certain times and less effective at others. However, through the rest of my day, when I feel stuck with a thought, I go back to visualizing opening my mental windows. Having a relaxed breath, I allow the forces of nature to assist the cleansing of mind.

If we respect Earth and Nature, they will in turn support us in ways far beyond our imagination.

So Breathe It.

January 16
THIS TOO SHALL PASS

There's usually an initial period in an upsetting experience when the uncomfortable or painful feelings will appear to be present indefinitely. As children we learn some ways to cope with hurt. As adults we have more options. Rather than choosing to medicate or avoid my feelings, I'm learning the value of acceptance. For me, this must happen before any sane and sober actions can take place. Here's how it often sounds in my mind as I make the effort to return to a compassionate place:

Breathe, just relax and breathe. Even though this hurts and is really uncomfortable, things could be a lot worse. Every pain in my life has eventually subsided. This will soon disappear like the rest. Thank You, God, for the truth that helps me come back to a sane and peaceful place within myself.

So Breathe It.

January 17
UNITED WE BREATHE

Do you realize that every living organism is breathing with you right now? Barring an emergency situation, this is always true. We all are breathing in harmony, all the time, everywhere. Is this not the essence of being one in truth? God has given us the gift of life, which is sustained on a minute-to-minute basis through our breathing.

How more can we appreciate this blessing than to take a few full, conscious breaths now? Try breathing in the thought "Thank You for my breath," and then breathe out "Amen, for a few more moments of sustained life."

Can you align a few of your own thoughts with your breathing? You might consider remembering and/or writing down a few of your favorites and using them on a regular basis.

By the Grace of God there go I. This very much includes my breathing during the next minute or two. "Grace" is not an esoteric or abstract concept by any means.

So Breathe It.

January 18
BELIEVING IS SEEING

Sometimes when my life and all its situations seem to be out of my control, it helps when I reach for something I have power over. Not only do we have the power to control our breathing, but when we do, it has a rippling effect throughout our entire being. A few moments of a relaxed focus on our breathing may not solve our challenges, but it certainly can reset the experience of the present moment.

When life is shouting at us, sometimes the gentlest supportive whisper can make all the difference. In this breath, I consciously choose to know that things are OK and will turn out for the best. I may not feel it, but I choose to know this.

Which is more truthful, "seeing is believing" or "believing is seeing"? God is, I am.

So Breathe It.

January 19
IN THE MOMENT

What does it really mean to make every moment count? Just by asking myself that question, my awareness is ricocheted into a more present place. Yes, in this moment, I allow myself to appreciate my breathing, my vision, my conscious stream of thoughts, and the hope of many more peaceful moments in my day. I now choose to get an uplifting moment by thinking of how close God is to me in this very moment. Really letting this truth in will transform how you can just be here now.

Infinite possibilities live in this moment for all of us.

So Breathe It.

January 20
MOVE A MUSCLE

Love, light, and life energy rush into all things when given a chance. There are three ways you can instigate the circulation of these things: change a thought, move a muscle, and practice improved conscious breathing. Just say "yes" to a thought that gives you a pleasant feeling, a thought of a sunset, a sunrise on the beach, or maybe a smile from someone you care about. Then reach your arms above your head or in front of you as you take a nice full breath. It's amazing the immediate shift that will happen when you do these simple and easy things. I think most of us may overlook the awesome benefits we can receive from doing some of these kinds of things several times through our days.

Today I will consciously shift my thinking, stretch my body, and breathe fully. The more I do this, the more benefits I will receive. Amen.

So Breathe It.

January 21
PRAYER BREATHING

Dear God, thank You for my life. Although I may not show my gratitude often, I vow to show You more and more by the little things I do. Let it be known that every time I take a full breath of Your air into my lungs, I thank You. When I exhale, I am completing the respiration process You designed so fantastically; thank You for that too.

Thank You for how Your oxygen moves from my lungs into my bloodstream and from there to every cell in my body. And thank You for how the oxygen molecules are then taken from the blood cells and given over to each cell.

I now thank You, God, for the return of carbon dioxide into the veins of my body, through which it will then travel all the way back to my lungs for my grateful exhale of the waste material. Thank You for the ease with which this happens throughout my whole lifetime.

So Breathe It.

January 22
WILLINGNESS

However much we pray for God's will to be done, it can be difficult to remember that we've been given the ability to get our own will in alignment with that of our creators. One of my own challenges is how to set aside my vested interest in having what I want, when I want it.

In this moment, as well as many more moments through our day, let us breathe in the idea of allowing our will to be one with that of the God of our understanding. Then breathe out a nice, full "so be it!"

When we notice tension, or a sense of forcing things, let's remember to let go and let the Universal Power Within work with us. With each available breath, we say: I'm willing to have our Wills be one.

When I don't really feel all that "willing," I open to the honest admission that I'm WILLING to be willing, to have our Wills be one.

So Breathe It.

January 23
WHAT'S SO, SO WHAT

For some of us, when we say our life is an "adventure," the mystery or the unknowingness of what lies ahead can bring up anxious feelings. When fear is present for us, let's get into the habit of taking a few breaths as we experience our feelings.

Once I accomplish the objective acknowledgment of what I'm feeling, I do my best to allow these feelings to be just "what's so." After I've taken any and all safe and appropriate action, I also do my best to defuse the grip of my fears by exhaling into the thought "so what." In the light of trust and faith it's much easier to allow that "so what" (which doesn't mean we don't care, but rather that we're in an accepting place) to resonate in my mind.

Thank You, Higher Power, for the endless ways I can use my thinking to let you guide and comfort me through this adventure of life. What's so is that I'm never alone. In accepting the past just as it is, I leave it with a "so what."

So Breathe It.

January 24
PROGRESS, NOT PERFECTION

What physical activity do you know of that does not require at least some heightened level of breathing? If you're a singer, you know just how important your lung capacity is. If you have some experience with yoga, you are very much aware of the part breathing plays in an effective session. Anyone who has a knowledge of the martial arts will swear that their breathing (tapping into their *Chi* or energy) is as important as any other skill they can perform.

Today's Daily Breath emphasizes the importance of increasing the awareness of our respiration through repetition. As with anything we practice, we improve. It would be hard not to guarantee that after 90 days of reading these messages and doing the simple breathing exercises, you would have drastically transformed the quality of your breathing. This in turn would have a direct positive impact on your health, well-being, and energy.

Please breathe a conscious full breath now. Each time you do that, you make a very real investment in the quantity and quality of the rest of your life.

Real prosperity lives within us. How rich we are is determined by the inner home in which we live. Breathing helps keep our space fresh and clean.

So Breathe It.

January 25
WAIT

I've created and use an acronym, WAIT. It stands for "Where Am I Tense?" Usually we know where in our bodies the tension lies because there is discomfort. But even if there is no obvious discomfort, after practicing the WAIT scan of my body, coupled with conscious breathing, I can usually find some low-grade chronic tension. It's not always in the usual neck and shoulder area. The jaw, toes, hands, pelvic area, and forehead are some of the places where, if I WAIT and see, I'll be able to release some or all of the contracted muscles.

One technique I use is a squeeze, breathe, and relax method. For instance, if I find I'm clenching my jaw, I'll slowly inhale as I gently tighten my jaw. I hold my breath with filled lungs and slightly tightened jaw for about five seconds, then release the contracted muscles and let the air out of my lungs with an unforced exhale. Sometimes I will add an affirmation, such as "I let go and let the life flow through my body." After repeating this process a few times I will notice a significant improvement.

WAIT can also stand for "What Am I Thinking?" This in turn can be a source of tension. The next time you hear or see the word "wait," let it trigger you to breathe, scan, shift, and release.

So Breathe It.

January 26
RELEASE

All of us have to rush to be somewhere or do things at certain points in our lives. Prioritizing becomes one of our most treasured skills during those times.

In order for our mind to be at peak functioning levels, it needs a full supply of nutrients brought by the circulatory system. When the rest of our body is tense, or in a contracted state, the muscles not only make the flow of blood to the brain more difficult but also make demands that take away from higher levels of functioning. This is where well-practiced breathing habits benefit us.

If we're in the habit of full and complete breathing patterns, when these patterns become restricted a red flag goes up, and we respond by automatically adjusting our breathing. As soon as we release the tight grip of the muscles in our neck, shoulders, and torso, we are freer to do our own rescue breathing.

In my release I shall find the Peace that goes beyond all understanding.

So Breathe It.

January 27
HONESTY

When we are faced with a decision of integrity, it can be difficult to take even a single full breath. Keeping agreements, whether they are with others or personal and private, can be among the most stress-producing experiences. One thing I know for sure, BREATHING WORKS! We almost always will have a moment or two to close our eyes and breathe in the hope of doing the next right thing for ourselves, which usually is right for others.

There's nothing I find more conducive to breathing easy than keeping an agreement, first and foremost one that supports my life and well-being.

In each breath we take, know the truth lives within.
Being honest to ourselves shows the highest integrity.
In this breath I rest, knowing my Higher Power patiently waits.
As I inhale I say "Let go," and as I exhale I say "Let God."

So Breathe It.

January 28
ENJOY NOT ENJOYING

I've done my best in training myself to immediately take a conscious breath or two when I hear upsetting or negative news. This gives me the chance to use my breathing and affirming truth with regard to staying spiritually connected in trying moments.

The act of a full inhale is expansive, which is a tangible action to counteract the tendency toward being contractive or tense in the light of adversity. You might consider 4-count breathing here: 4 seconds on the inhale, and 4 seconds exhaling.

I also recommend you make a list on paper, on a device, and/or in your mind. List all the times when you notice your breathing is restricted or limited. This list will help you be more aware of when it would work best to adjust your breathing.

Remember, this program is about conditioning us to have better breathing. This exercise could be viewed as using Principle 4 (taking stock or inventory) as to where and when our breathing has been affected.

It's taught in Rebirthing to breathe into each feeling. If we're not enjoying something, breathe and do our best at enjoying NOT enjoying. If then we're still unable to do that, breathe into the possibility of finding enjoyment in not enjoying, not enjoying. Get what we're saying?

So Breathe It.

January 29
TAKING NO POSITION

Clearly we have judgments, evaluations, and/or opinions about every situation we are involved in. An evolved being can step back and notice how he or she is coloring a given event. To assist me in letting go of how I think things should be, I've learned certain thoughts I can have during interactions: "I can see the world differently." "It's OK not to not know what's best." "I can just be in this situation without trying to fix or change things."

Knowing I never know God's plan, I can however be true to my beliefs as I let go and let God.

"God, I may or may not be accurate with my perception here. As I now breathe, I allow my thoughts and feelings to just be as they are so I may have a sacred few moments when You take over, as I cease trying to force or make things happen. God, I know when I accomplish taking no position, I become receptive to Your blessings of benevolence, love, and often forgiveness. Thank You for the innate ability to step back and open to Your will being done. Amen."

So Breathe It.

January 30
PRINCIPLE BREATHING

When I notice my breathing is short, strained, or limited in any way, I'm reminded of Principle 1. Here's how I would reword the principle to be appropriate for breathing: "I declare that I need help with my breathing, that it is becoming very difficult to keep my breathing deep and relaxed."

Officially that's how it would sound; however, in reality, the actual thought may be this: "My breathing is out of whack. Breathe, Scott. Everything will be better handled if you can continue to just breathe."

We have now used Principle 1 for several situations pertaining to health and well-being. The truth is this principle can be used in any situation where we declare help is wanted and/or needed.

"God, I can't find my keys, and I need help here." God might answer through my thoughts: "Breathe, Scott. When you're ready and willing, you'll remember where they are."

So Breathe It.

January 31
GIVING AND RECEIVING

By this point we can assume that an inhale may be aligned with positive and life-affirming things—phrases, words, visions, or even just feelings. When we want to take in energy, we inhale. Likewise, whatever we want to release or expel, we breathe out. Yes, we've used positive affirmations for both parts of our breathing. However, as we align energy with respiration (taking in fresh and pushing out used and toxic air) it works well to do the same with our creative visualizing.

I breathe in thoughts of healing and breathe out illness. In with Love, out with fear. I open to positive people and see toxic ones being pushed away.

Truth is; untruth has no real power. Being filled with light, there can be no darkness.

So Breathe It.

February 1
HOLD IN YOUR BREATH

I have been submerged underwater for an uncomfortable amount of time. Apparently I have swum a bit too deep for my available oxygen reserves. I have panicky thoughts as I frantically swim toward the surface. It's close; I can see my salvation. Then the question creeps into my mind. Can I make it? Just as quickly the whisper comes from within: "Don't give up, keep going."

My hands reach the surface. Then I gasp in the life-saving air. As I continue my elated breaths of life, my only thought is one of thankfulness for this air I am able to freely breathe.

How true is the saying that "We don't really appreciate what we have until we do not have it anymore."

Our current experiences may be different, but we are all sooner or later faced with the need to "come up for air."

So Breathe It.

February 2
READY, AIM, FIRE

Watching a golf tournament I was pleasantly surprised when I heard the announcer (a famous PGA champion) describe his putting technique. He said that as he moved the putter backward he would take a full breath in, and as he began his stroke forward he'd exhale. How wise is that method? It can be used in almost every sport humans participate in. Can you think about the sports you might play and see how it would work to align your breathing with actions?

In a more practical day-to-day use for myself, I consciously use my breathing as I get out of bed in the morning. Before I move, I breathe in, and as I breathe out I turn on my side and use my arms to push up to a sitting position. After a few more conscious breaths I stand up on an exhale and go my way.

The essence of "ready, aim, fire" has countless applications in life. Inhale/ready/exhale, inhale/aim/exhale, inhale/fire/exhale.

So Breathe It.

February 3
WELLATIVITY'S SIGN OF THE CROSS

One day I was watching someone making the sign of the cross. As I understand what is meant by performing this action, I can align with blessing and protection. However, I have always wanted to come up with a more New-Age action to symbolize much of the same essence.

It came to me one day. Wellativity's action will be as such:

With open hands facing upward to the sky, I take a deep breath in. I put one hand on top of the other open palm and then pull both hands toward my heart. Beginning my exhale, I extend my outstretched hands away from my body at the body-center level. In essence this symbolizes the taking in of the blessings /protection/ life energy of the Universe and (while synchronizing with my breathing) then offering it all back out to the world.

I breathe in God's energy of love and unconditionally channel it to all who are in need of it. Amen.

So Breathe It.

February 4
BREATHE IN TO PRINCIPLE TWO

"Came to understand that a Power within ourselves would guide us back to the joy of breathing."

The wonderful thing about reading or speaking this Principle (translated for breathing) is that by the time most of us have finished reading, saying, or just remembering it, we have already demonstrated its truth.

Our breathing process is intriguing. Even if limited, it will continue for life. The fantastic thing is the unlimited uses we have for this gift. Top on the list of amazing aspects to my breathing is that by reading about, hearing, or watching someone breathing, I will automatically shift to taking full and improved breaths.

To emphasize the simplicity of working with the Principles, it sounds or looks like this:

Principle One: "I'm noticing I am not breathing well."
Principle Two: "Thank You for returning me to the joy of breathing."

It can help us to breathe easier if we know there's a Power just waiting for our openness to restore us to optimal health and well-being. As children, most of us believed in magic. As adults, we are being urged to return to the innocence that comes with youthful belief and faith.

So Breathe It.

February 5
MAKE THE CHOICE

"Made a choice to allow the source of Power within to improve our breathing throughout our lives."

Considering that you are reading a Daily Breath now and possibly have chosen to do the full 90-day breathing conditioning program, it's a given that to a certain degree, you are practicing Principle Three.

As with breathing, we can be utilizing positive tools without being aware of it. However, you might consider using Principle Three toward breathing in a regular and a conscious way, possibly during your prayer and meditation times. The point is to make the choice to allow help, as often and as deeply as possible.

Following is a Third-Principle prayer for breathing:

God, I now turn over to You all that has gotten in my way of healthy breathing. I allow the reminders to breathe into my awareness as often as You would wish. Thank You, God, for giving me the choice to allow you to help me breathe in the life You've freely given to me. Amen.

So Breathe It.

February 6
WHAT'S IN STOCK

"Looked deeply and honestly as we took stock of our breathing."

This translation will mean different things to different people. Making a list will help you to be thorough. When you take this inventory, you may be surprised at what you remember. Everything you recall that relates to your breathing throughout your life belongs in this inventory, from limited lung capacity due to smoking, to a near-drowning experience, to pneumonia, to asthma, to all respiratory conditions.

At the very least you will have a new sense of appreciation for what breathing means for you. This may also remind you of things you did not put on your original Principle 4 list.

It's important to remember here that by reading today's Daily Breath you are working on your breathing conditioning program. The repetition of bringing up how and what your breathing is for you results in your building an improved consciousness around the most important tool for your health and well-being in every moment of your life.

Each of our experiences and conditions holds tremendous value. We would be wise to not let our judgments dilute or invalidate what we've gathered throughout life.

So Breathe It.

February 7
THE POWER OF SPEECH

"Told to the Power within, to ourselves, and to another person whom we trusted, the truth about the exact conditions of our breathing."

Not that a breathing condition is something many of us would put much energy into keeping secret, but once the truth is spoken we can then eliminate the possibility of our spending valuable energy on maintaining secrets on any level. As was alluded to in my first book, *Wellativity: In-Powering Wellness Through Communication*, we are only as sick as our secrets.

Just like the relief of getting things off our chest in therapy or in a meeting, it holds true that we'll breathe easier when we speak the truth about our respiratory history.

"Oh my God, I can't believe you smoked cigarettes! I've never told anyone this before but since you confided in me, I want you to know that I've hidden the fact that I still occasionally smoke. I've never told anyone that! Believe it or not, now that I've told you, it feels as if I'm breathing easier."

The truth be told, I'm not nearly as bad as I thought, nor as special as I fantasized.

So Breathe It.

February 8
THE ULTIMATE PARTNER

"Became completely ready and willing to have the source of life within work with us toward healing our breathing."

Let's make no mistake about it, knowing that a Power greater than ourselves is helping us to heal in itself improves our breathing. Again, let there be no misunderstanding about what it may take for us to become completely "ready and willing" to let support into our lives. "I can take care of myself," "I'll figure things out on my own," and "I don't need any help" are things we've all said at one time or another. These are beliefs that require a closed and resistant way of being. True surrender to opening ourselves to help, although we may not understand it, takes a lot of courage, strength, and trust.

One thing I've noticed almost without exception is that when I let go of my willfulness, I not only breathe a sigh of relief but have the peace of mind that comes with being partners with the very Best.

So Breathe It.

February 9
HUMILITY

"With a sense of humility, asked the Power within to help restore us to a place of healthy breathing."

Once we've accomplished the readiness and willingness that was suggested in Principle Six, humbly asking the Power within can be as effortless as our next breath. In the context of translating steps and Principles, at this point we might even consider that "with a sense of humility, affirming the Power within can and will help restore our healthy breathing." For me, having just taken a few full breaths while writing these words has demonstrated the effectiveness in affirming or saying yes to the Power's help.

This concept may assist you in shifting your whole context of what praying is and what it can be used for in the restoration of your health and vitality. Prayer then becomes an act of getting in alignment with what your Higher Power needs of you.

I humbly say yes to what Your Will is for me, God. Thank You, for I humbly know in my heart that my healing has already begun.

So Breathe It.

February 10
WILLING TO RESTORE

"Made a list of all the destructiveness that we had contributed to our bodies that has been expressed by unhealthy breathing. Then became willing to compassionately take restorative actions to all involved, except when to do so would be harmful or unacceptable to ourselves or others."

This differs from what we've done in the Fourth and Fifth Principles, in that we're making a list that includes not only us but others. It might also be wise to note that the key phrase here is that we "became willing." This should help all of us breathe easier! No part of being willing requires action, condemnation, or judgments of any form.

If there's something in your throat or lungs that's obstructing your breathing, you get it out by coughing. Likewise, if there's something, whether it be mental or emotional, that's making you tense, thus making it hard for you to breathe, first acknowledge it, then deal with it.

Breathing better and easier is certainly an end result from cleaning house.

So Breathe It.

February 11
ACTION

"Took direct action in healing our breathing wherever it felt right, making sure to keep safety as a priority."

I recommend you understand Principle Nine completely. If there's any question on how to apply this Principle to the healing of your breathing, go back and review the chapter in *Wellativity* that dealt with working the Ninth Principle.

For now, this can be as simple as taking a few full breaths, not lighting up your next cigarette (or cutting down), remembering to take prescribed medicine for your lungs, calling your trusted support and making a plan, etc.

When generating the energy to fix, restore, or clean up something, let's remember the importance of moderation. Another way to put this is: Easy Does It.

God, in each one of my breaths I know You're guiding me to do the next right healing action. How comforting it is to experience this effortless truth every time I breathe in Your gift of life. I show my gratitude for this blessing by doing my best and leaving the rest.

So Breathe It.

February 12
LIVING IN THE QUESTION

"Continued to question what was working or not, and when adjustments were needed, made them, as nonjudgmentally as possible."

Principle Ten needs no rewording. It can be applied to any area in our lives that needs maintaining and/or improving.

Whether it be several times in a minute, an hour, or a day, keeping an inquiring consciousness around our breathing yields infinite benefits. Let's remember that our breathing is the bridge between our mental, physical, emotional, and spiritual worlds.

When we set out to make needed adjustments (even as simple as taking a few full conscious breaths), we connect with our Higher Power. When we maintain healthy oxygen levels, which also works in conjunction with balancing our stress/tension levels, our brains not only work better but are more able to be channels of the life-affirming energy that keeps us healthier.

Living in the question of how, when, where, and why to make improvements is certainly where God came from when creation was conceived.

So Breathe It.

February 13
BREATHING CREATES MIRACLES

"Sought through our breathing to stay consciously connected to the Energy of Life within us, asking ourselves to remain completely open to its guidance and to focus on our willingness to act from a loving place rather than from fear."

Saying that we're seeking through our breathing to stay consciously connected to the Energy of Life within us is not finding other ways to connect but rather using our breathing as the focus toward accomplishing our objective.

Meditation, chanting, praying, yoga, tai chi, even most aerobic exercise are activities that serve and are served by healthy and effective breathing patterns.

This Principle above all others chooses to act from love rather than from fear. With respect to the subject of improved breathing, experiencing either love or fear has been known to take our breath away. Most of us will find ourselves with the choice either to contract and resist or to expand and breathe. Practicing the Eleventh Principle will help you deal with life on life's terms.

We breathe in love and breathe out fear. Once we've accepted the ultimate reality of God's love, fear becomes the stranger here. Thank You, God, for the time and space for each of us to freely choose from the highest to the lowest and all in between.

So Breathe It.

February 14
PROOF OF THE PUDDING

"Having had a deep transformation as the result of these Principles, we live by example and unconditionally practice these truths to the best of our abilities throughout our lives."

Principle Twelve says a lot if we consider it only from the simple act of breathing. If you look at this Principle as an opportunity to share something of value that you've been working with, it then takes on a different meaning.

Let's say you make a note as a reminder to breathe, and someone else sees it on your desk or refrigerator and takes a deep breath as a result. This is Principle 12 in action. In addition, the person may say "what a great idea," and then pass it on to others. They in turn do the same, and so on. What a difference you've made in living by example with very little effort. Conscious breathing is contagious.

Still another way of reinforcing for yourself the valuable work here is to talk about it with others. What, how, and why working on your breathing has worked for you is a good place to start.

God, because of You, I can now light the way as Your beacon of wisdom. In Your breath of life, I breathe, rejoice, and thank You. Amen.

So Breathe It.

February 15
FORGIVENESS

I once heard someone say that the essence of forgiveness is a giving-way to the flow of life. Physiologically speaking, there's no better "giving-way" to the flow of life than breathing. However, we humans require a lot when it comes to forgiving. The emotional effects on one who holds firmly onto being unforgiving can be fear, resistance, and/or resentment. In the context of health and well-being, these emotions are constrictive. Even when I have trouble forgiving a certain action, I do my best to return home to an expansive and inclusive consciousness.

When I'm willing to be willing to forgive, I breathe better.
When I'm willing to forgive, I breathe better.
When I forgive, I breathe better.
When I'm forgiven, I breathe better.
It's always within my reach to breathe better.

So Breathe It.

February 16
PARTNERS

Having a supportive partner in almost any endeavor will yield better results than if you work alone. What if you were to ask someone to do this breathing conditioning program with you? If that's not workable for you, how about asking a trusted person to discuss your experience and progress with you on a daily basis until you complete the initial 90 days? On an even lighter level of support, making it a point to share what and how you're doing with your program can be immensely supportive.

The funny thing about putting into words what you're learning through training and conditioning is that it becomes more real for you and for others. Moreover, it is rewarding to know you've possibly supported another person in living a healthier and longer life.

The way we all are equal is that we all breathe. It's a very cool feeling to breathe, knowing we're all doing this one thing together, as one, despite our differences.

So Breathe It.

February 17
PEACE

One of the most peaceful experiences I can have is to watch my girlfriend breathing as she quietly sleeps. For that matter, even watching my cats sleep and breathe has a relaxing, meditative effect on me. Then, closing my eyes, I place my hand on the sleeper next to me and connect with my own breathing. Each rise and fall of my hand is a tangible affirmation of breathing, connectedness, and peace. If there's no one near me, I sometimes put my hand just below my ribs where my diaphragm muscle is and feel my own breathing.

Thank You, God, for those moments when I experience a deep peaceful connectedness with ones You've also created. In Your light of peace I am ever reminded that we are all truly one.

So Breathe It.

February 18
POWER

Taking a deep breath is essential in the moments when we realize that we're powerless over certain people, places, and things.

Is this not critical in being powerful? Understanding and accepting our weaknesses is the first step in gaining real power. Truth be told, our most powerful tool is our mind. It can train us to use our other God-given tools for powerful living. Our mind will remind us to breathe, if we program it to do this. THAT'S IT, PROGRAMMING!

I breathe in this truth.
I use everything I can to program my mind to use the awesome tool of breathing.
I say yes to my power in this breath.
I say no to doubting my power in this next breath.
Saying yes to my power is as easy as breathing in air.

So Breathe It.

February 19
FIRST WE BREATHE

Our first impulse on this earth is to gasp for air. And for all who have gone to the beyond, their last act in life was a final gasp for air. I say this not to dismay you but to bring you back to the preciousness of something that's been intimately close within you from the first day of your life. No thought, no person, nothing (aside from God) will remain with you as your breathing will until your last moment on this earth. Therefore, is not breathing your very best lifetime friend? Considering that we've been granted the ability to control, improve, and enjoy this "best friend" of ours, wouldn't it make sense for us to give our breathing as much conscious time as possible? What we give love and attention to, like a friend, will grow to have a closer and deeper meaning for us.

Sometimes I laugh when I hear the common phrase "take one day at a time." Not that the statement is not infinitely wise, but there have been many times when I could have only hoped to reach for my next breath, let alone the end of an entire day!

So Breathe It.

February 20
A SIGH OF RELIEF

Breathing a sigh of relief is comforting. Why is it, then, that when we are anxious or afraid, we tend to hold our breath? Is it some primal instinct to do this? Are we instinctively trying to be as quiet as possible so as not to be found and attacked? Maybe it's some collective belief passed down through the ages that if we hold our breath, we can somehow slow down or prevent an undesirable event.

Whatever the reasons, after we practice actions over and over, they become automatic and habitual. The best way to change habits is to practice other behaviors to replace the old ones. The truth that we have a choice to change our habits should definitely help us to breathe a sigh of relief.

We always have a choice. If only to take a deep breath, sometimes that's enough.

So Breathe It.

February 21
A RELAXED FOCUS

Allowing the value of having a relaxed focus into our minds has all kinds of benefits for us. Meditation, sports, prayer, writing, painting, all require a certain degree of relaxing and effort at the same time. It's much the same if we just notice something with no beliefs or feelings added. When I become aware of my breathing, I often see it as poor or not good. I then do my best to realize that when I just notice my breathing, it corrects itself; in turn, if I permit myself to prolong my watching of the inhales and exhales, I increase the nature of my relaxed focus.

All I have to do is become aware of Your presence, God, and I relax in the assurance that comes with focusing on Your loving Power within my being. Thank you.

So Breathe It.

February 22
PROPHETIC BREATHING

It's awesome to realize that even the prophets breathed. Jesus, Moses, Mohammad, Gandhi, the Buddha, and countless others all breathed to live. In addition they too enjoyed and faced the challenges that are part of our human breathing process.

Prophet or peasant, breathing is the same for all who ever were, and ever will be. Is this yet one more sign that humans were designed equal?

I pray for each of us to find the common ground for which we all breathe and have our being.
I pray that we can reach for the aspects of being human that unite us all.
In our prayer let the gift of breath guide us back to our true home. Amen.

So Breathe It.

February 23
ROAD RAGE

In our culture, "road rage" ranks high in the more dangerous of our reactive behaviors. Enough cannot be said of the importance of getting even one full breath in the midst of this high speed anger. In those few moments, we could conceivably save more than one life. The point I want to emphasize is that practicing this breathing conditioning program could enable us to get in the habit (without necessarily thinking about it) of pausing in our most critical times.

When we are "seeing red," yield for one inhale of blue, or green, or even violet. Even if we don't feel it, let's see ourselves exhaling red. Using these visualizations is like the breathing conditioning program as well. The more we practice the tool of visualizing, the more impact and value we will get from it.

I breathe in the healing color of blue/green, and breathe out the red of my anger, rage, and hatred.
Higher Power, please lift these potentially dangerous thoughts and feelings from my mind and body. I am now willing to let go and let You help me in my next calm, sane, and life-affirming choices.

So Breathe It.

February 24
SELF-RESCUE BREATHING

Anyone who has dealt with depression knows how difficult just breathing can be. As in our more intense moments of emotion, it is of great importance to now give ourselves a few rescue breaths. The potential weight on our shoulders and chest from deep sadness can suffocate us, if we allow it.

Saying "I can do this," that is, increase the depth of your breathing, might be the best you can do in a challenging experience. When giving CPR rescue breathing, one must force air into the person in need. A similar technique may work for you when pulling in air is difficult. Force whatever air you have in your lungs out. Your body will do the rest by gasping in your next breath. As always, be firm but not too forceful with this technique.

There is a rescuer for all of us. Most often we are the ones that need to reach for the extended helping hand.

So Breathe It.

February 25
TOO MUCH AIR

Hyperventilating, or taking in too much oxygen, can accompany extreme fear, trauma, and anxiety. The technique to balance or counteract this is to breathe into a paper bag for a short period. If you find yourself hyperventilating (experiencing periods of rapid short breathing), and you don't have a paper bag, you might try cupping your hands over your mouth and nose while leaving just enough room for air to come and go. Your hands should block enough carbon dioxide (which is what we exhale and which can help during hyperventilation).

Part of this breathing conditioning program is being aware of the many different aspects of our breathing. Reading about our breath automatically helps improve how you're breathing; in addition, these facts will contribute to your safety and possibly your survival.

So Breathe It.

February 26
SMOKING

I often speak of creating the desire for healthier things. Cultivating a new consciousness is the wise first step before forcing behavioral changes. I had been doing this unknowingly years ago with regard to breathing. Participating in yoga, rebirthing (a therapeutic technique using breathing as the main modality), and meditation courses were some of my consciousness building.

However, my still being a smoker back then presented a conflict to say the least. Without going into much detail, I had a breakthrough in consciousness around smoking and breathing. Until I could stop this unhealthy habit, I was going to make the effort during the smoking of a cigarette to stay focused on my breathing, not just the sensation that came from inhaling smoke, but the complete act of breathing before, during, and after each breath of smoke. As time went on I became more and more appreciative of what breathing was to me. Needless to say, working with the consciousness around all types of breathing very much assisted me in the letting go of the smoking habit.

With regard to this topic, "it's easier to ride the horse in the direction it's going" (one of my favorite aphorisms) does not mean to judge our behaviors but rather to see where they are leading us, which can make our healthier transitions much less negative.

So Breathe It.

February 27
YAWNING

By definition, yawning is a deep inhalation and exhalation with an involuntary opening wide of the mouth. The suggestion is that it is from tiredness or boredom. For myself, boredom is a suspect cause at best. On the other hand, tiredness makes complete physiological sense. As with all muscles, the diaphragm (muscle for breathing) when fatigued will have subpar involuntary performance. With enough subpar breathing over a long-enough duration, the department in our brain responsible for maintaining a minimal amount of oxygen for survival will kick in or jump-start larger inhalations.

Thank God for this design! Without it we could very well suffocate every time we grew tired. So the next time you feel the need to yawn, welcome it; if someone asks you if you're bored you might just tell them there's nothing boring about survival.

So Breathe It.

February 28
THE SCENT OF A PERSON

I was sitting in a meeting with about 30 people very early one morning. I found it more and more difficult to breathe due to the amount of cologne worn by one of the men next to me. This, mixing in with a few other perfumes in the room, had me working Principle One: Managing my Health, which was becoming very difficult. Step One, "being powerless" over a substance, was in my consciousness as well.

There's not much I can do about this, other than get up and leave. What's the reality here, Scott? I'm not going to die. I have a burning sensation in my eyes, throat, and mouth, but I'm not in danger. OK, so if I just breathe through my mouth, I can pay attention to what's being said. Good, short, steady breathing will do it. "God, does this intrusive, oppressive, and confronting way of being within crowds ever get easier?"

Answer: "Yes, no, maybe."

So Breathe It.

February 29
LAMAZE

Where can we find a more profound example of using our breathing as a tool as in childbirth? The technique has multiple benefits for both of the partners. For the expectant mother, this deep-breathing technique helps her to keep oxygen flowing through her body and her baby's body, and it helps her deal with the pain of giving birth.

Let's address the partner as the "father-to-be," although we know it can be many different people in the supportive position. Yes, the primary focus is on the one giving birth, but if we look at what often causes the father-to-be to pass out, it would be lack of oxygenated blood to his brain. This being said, the Lamaze technique can help the father stay conscious and be part of the success, rather than a part of a potential distraction or problem.

Your tools and gifts for all events seem to be unending and ever evolving. Thank You again, God.

So Breathe It.

March 1
PLANE BREATHING

There are few more unpleasant (and possibly unhealthy) prolonged breathing experiences than air travel. The close quarters along with processed air for hours at a time speaks for itself. It's not likely to happen anytime soon, but wouldn't it be special if airlines offered optional oxygen mask use for an additional cost? I'd definitely pay the extra charge.

Practically speaking, we can stack the deck in our favor by doing a few things prior to a flight. First, have an extended deep breathing session in a fresh-air environment. Second, consume oxygen-rich foods such as fruits and vegetables (that are appropriate to any physical condition you might have) shortly before take-off. Third, an infusion of immune system building supplements (again, medically approved for you) could be helpful. Last, but definitely not least: prayer, meditation, and breathing exercises during the voyage.

Thank You, God, for the air I breathe. Although I can be distracted by some discomforts, I know You've always been there guiding and protecting me through every journey. THANK YOU.

So Breathe It.

March 2
ASTHMA

Anyone with asthma, or any similar respiratory condition, knows well the value of consistent easy breathing. If you ever want a powerful prayer toward breathing, people who have asthma probably have many they could share with you.

Growing up I had the opportunity to witness a neighboring family who almost all suffered from asthma. Experiencing any of them having an attack brought home to me the very meaning of being powerless.

I currently have some friends and clients who have respiratory conditions. My first and foremost supportive action is to always make sure they have their inhalers on hand. You might be surprised at how many times a gentle reminder to take that precious tool of life with them has helped them. Other than that, let us pray.

Not usually sure of Your plan, God, I trust my friends are always in Your best care. I do my best to get my worry out of the way and surround them with the light of Your healing life. Thank You for my free and easy breathing. In each of my breaths I affirm the magnificence of this gift we all have. Amen.

March 3
CPR

Cardio Pulmonary Resuscitation is essentially "breathing life" into a person. Unless you're one of the relatively few who know how to perform CPR, you won't have this miraculous experience of literally pushing life back into a person. There are very few things as intimate and sacred as using the gift of your breath/life to not only keep someone alive but also help the people who love and care for that individual in need.

If you see the quality of our breathing as critical on many levels, you will have ample opportunities to share the value of these readings. Working with the Daily Breath breathing conditioning program is not only training you to increase your awareness of your breathing but also enabling you to help others in their resuscitation. Let's call this work your Breathing Awareness Resuscitation, training course. Every time you share this training with others, you are actively administering Breathing Awareness Resuscitation. In addition, we are following the principle that by helping others we increase the intrinsic value for ourselves.

God, help me to help myself to remember that giving and receiving are one in truth and that I can't keep it unless I give it away.

So Breathe It.

March 4
SNORING

What can we say about this breathing condition? If you're not the one doing it, someone snoring next to you or even in another room can bring up some intense feelings. Pinching their nose closed may work for a little while, but usually not for very long. Pushing, bouncing, loud sighing have all been things I've attempted. However, in the end it's up to the snorer to find and use a remedy.

For the innocent bystander it can be a wise time to put all our spiritual/metaphysical/therapeutic techniques to work. Other than using headphones or earplugs, sometimes it works for me to go into a meditative mode.

So it's very possible that I may be kept awake all night. I know the old saying that what I resist shall persist. It's not so much the snoring that I'm resisting, but my feelings and thoughts. What's the opportunity here, Scott? Breathe. Breathe right into your feelings. Surrender to what is so. Thank You, God, for I am well enough myself to have only a minor problem such as someone snoring. Amen.

So Breathe It.

March 5
SINUS CONGESTION

When your sinuses are congested, whether due to a virus, allergies, or a structural blockage, the idea of free and clear breathing takes on a meaning different from what most people have. More than most, you will appreciate what oxygen you can receive.

Breathing with your mouth can present many difficulties, especially in a public setting. But you must do what you need to do in order to survive. Being upfront and honest with people around you may not always be appropriate. When it is, this can at least put you a bit more at ease.

I may not understand why I have this condition, God, but I'll do my best to take care of what's mine to do. My prayer is one of healing. I affirm my right to health, and in the same breath I humbly ask for my full and complete restoration of health. Thank You. Amen.

So Breathe It.

March 6
RESPIRATOR

Staying in the context of building our awareness of or consciousness about breathing includes looking at every dimension of respiration. Breathing assisted by a respirator is probably the most artificial way of breathing we have. However, if it were keeping you or a loved one alive, would you not be eternally grateful?

When I see technology used with breathing, I'm not only in awe but also brought to a place of amazement about how God and man have worked together in creating fantastic devices such as the respirator to help us breathe.

Here's something for you to think about: how many things we have that assist our breathing. Medicine, surgery, technology, fitness, and well-being practices should all be included.

When we feel like technology is replacing humanity, consider where we would be without it.

So Breathe It.

March 7
SMELLING THE FLOWERS

"Take time to smell the flowers" can mean many things. It tells us to use our breathing to enjoy something pleasant. Most will also understand this phrase to mean that we should slow down, there are things we may be missing in life, and if we were to pause to take a breath now and then, it would do us good. Let's remember that our breathing is not just designed for survival. I'm sure that in God's creation of human breathing, the many levels we would use this amazing capacity to smell and to breathe were considered.

Thank You, God, for all that breathing coupled with our sense of smell brings us. Let us learn to develop this sense all the way into the realm of spirituality. What a gift!

So Breathe It.

March 8
SCUBA DIVING

Is it not incredible that we have created a way to enter a world completely different from our familiar one just by strapping a tank filled with compressed oxygen onto our backs?

Until relatively recent times, this world within our own world was alien to mankind. Technology once again has been coupled with one of our senses and our need to breathe. The equipment made for us to see underwater (goggles) was not even close to what it takes to be able to breathe under water.

The deeper the water, the more pressure exerted on the torso, the more effort-filled the breathing. Here's an idea for when you feel the pressures of life, which, indeed, can also make breathing much more difficult. Let *Wellativity's Daily Breath* be your oxygen tank. The messages can be your reminder to breathe, even when your pressures seem oppressive.

I assert to you that the more you practice conscious breathing, the better you will maintain poise in all situations. No matter what the heights or the depths of your life's journey, coming back within, to your breathing, can and will help in all situations.

So Breathe It.

March 9
EMISSIONS

There's no way around it. Living in our society, you have breathed and will continue to breathe air that is tainted with various toxins. The fact is, too much toxic air and we physically cannot survive. At the other end of the spectrum, if after spending your life in a relatively toxin-free environment you go to a polluted urban place you will indeed have more adverse reactions than the acclimated, because your defenses have not been built up as have those of the city dwellers.

The point is to look for the silver lining, or concentrate on what is positive in a not-so-positive situation. For instance, you find yourself next to a bus that has blown its carbon monoxide in your face. After you get away from the dangerous emissions, you naturally will breathe in as much fresh air as possible.

My recommended thought, after you've reached safety is: "Thank God my respiratory system is designed to get rid of the toxic debris as quickly as possible!"

Dear God, I know I am powerless over so much that comes into my lungs. I know You've granted me the serenity to accept this fact. I also know You freely give me the courage to change the things I can. In addition I'm endowed with the wisdom to know what I can and cannot change. Amen.

So Breathe It.

March 10
RESETTING

One breath, that's it, one breath is all it takes to reset our perception. Magic, miracles, gifts, all can be initiated by our breathing. In this breath I let go, I relax my tense belly, I drop my shoulders, and again I breathe. When I release a contracting muscle, it's enabled to replenish the muscle fibers with nutrients that allow the muscle to function. The same holds true for our brains. Unless there is enough blood flow (carrying nutrients and oxygen) to the brain, it does not work properly. So when I breathe, stretch, and breathe again, I am literally resetting so much in my entire being. Do we not build into many of our machines a circuit breaker/power surge protector/reset buttons? Why would we not have the same capacity built into us?

It might not seem like very much, but if we condition ourselves to check and reset often, it will have tremendous benefits over a long period.

So Breathe It.

March 11
COLOR COORDINATION

The technique of using colors with therapeutic visualizing, affirming, and breathing is not new. The bottom line to this is that a person chooses a few colors he or she likes, and a few they do not prefer. Now we are told to breathe in the ones we like, and breathe out the ones we do not. Taking this a step further, we find a spot or body part for which we want healing and breathe in the color we like most. Likewise, we see the color we have least preference for and see ourselves breathing that color away from the area, taking with it unhealthy cells and bacteria. Ultimately we see the debris being exhaled out.

This is an extremely valuable technique because it aligns our creative thinking with our tangible and repetitive breathing. The energy involved with creativity and physical function are different, but when they're coordinated, in that pairing more power is generated toward healing.

Maybe learning to coordinate our own internal energies, in the common purpose of healing, is a secret in healing our lives. Hearing a soloist can be a beautiful experience, but hearing a symphony . . . well, need I say more?

So Breathe It.

March 12
BODY ODORS

I'm often intrigued by how most people don't find their own body odors offensive. I certainly don't. Could it be that because we've been breathing them in for so long, there's some sort of familiarity principle going on? With my two cats, I found their odors were not so pleasant at first, but as time went by, I grew to like even some of the ones most would not. The same holds true for humans I've grown close to. Over time my reactions change.

A thought you might consider: When you smell an unpleasant body odor, is it that you really don't like breathing it in, or is it more because it is unfamiliar? Of course some will always be more offensive than others, but the trick is to see if we can lessen the intensity so as to be able to breathe just a bit easier.

Are my judgments and evaluations imprisoning me and how I see the world? Can I just let things be the way they are for even one full breath?

So Breathe It.

March 13
CLAUSTROPHOBIA

Anyone who has experienced claustrophobia knows exactly how it affects their breathing. Having felt it myself, I'm aware that the primary feeling is one of not being able to breathe, or of suffocation. Truly, the only plausible antidote is to relax and breathe. However, with claustrophobia, that's easier said than done. Again, I believe that the regular practice of conscious breathing can play a positive role if and when we find ourselves in such an anxiety-ridden position.

God, if I am not to live through this experience, I shall go with one last attempt to breathe Your life into my lungs. I surrender my resistance to the inevitable. You've granted me the wisdom to know what I can change and what I can't. In my gratitude for this, I shall take one more breath, and even another if You should so allow it. Amen.

So Breathe It.

March 14
INTIMATE BREATHING

Among my favorite ways of breathing is intimate breathing. This may or may not involve anything of a sexual nature. Of course people do not have many opportunities to be physically closer than during sex. The art of Tantra often uses aligned breathing for a heightened experience between partners. The essence of all this is synchronizing energies, from mental to emotional to sexual and, ultimately, to a spiritual bonding.

A more contemporary and practical use of intimate breathing for me is when I'm lying, sitting, or "spooning" with the one I love. Sometimes it's difficult to maintain synchronized breathing for very long, but I usually can benefit from 5 or 10 aligned breaths with my partner and do my best to not be critical about the duration.

In each breath I breathe with this loved one is just one more moment in which I am free to see Your grace and in which I can bond with You, me, and her. There is no greater moment I have yet known. I pray to have many more. Thank You. Amen.

So Breathe It.

March 15
LAUGHING

Did you ever hear someone say they laughed so much that they could hardly catch their breath? And what would laughter sound like without the accompaniment of breathing? The last thing we want to do is get too much into anything but just laughing when it's happening. However, the next time you have the good fortune of having a good laugh, when you're done, take a full deep breath. If even once you giggle, then become aware of your breathing, *Wellativity's Daily Breath* will be working. For that matter, regardless of whether it's laughing or any other topic concerning the awareness of your breathing, if your awareness is elevated, your breathing conditioning program, indeed, will be benefiting you.

Laugh, and the whole world laughs with you. Breathe, and the whole Universe breathes with you.

So Breathe It.

March 16
THE HEIMLICH MANEUVER

As with any type of rescue breathing, you are taking someone's life in your hands. If you don't already know how to assist someone who is choking from an obstruction to their airway (the Heimlich Maneuver), I highly recommend taking a CPR class in which you'll learn rescue breathing as well as the Heimlich. Until then, be aware that restaurants are required to display a poster showing how it's to be performed. I'm not an advocate of using fear as a manipulation, but I would recommend taking one of these courses on the off chance someone near you could one day need your help. I know I'd hope for this expertise from a person if I needed assistance to breathe my next breath.

Another benefit from taking one of these courses is that it would give you the opportunity to stay in the appreciation and consciousness of how precious our breathing is. This, as well, is what *Wellativity's Daily Breath* is all about.

Playing God is one thing, but working with God in helping another to breathe is quite another.

So Breathe It.

March 17
TALKING

We're addressing as many things that incorporate our breathing process as possible. Talking is no exception. As a matter of fact, if you were to try to talk without first taking a breath, you would be hard pressed to make much more than a barely audible sound.

It would be unrealistic to think that every time we began to talk, we would have a heightened experience of appreciation for our breathing. But every once in a while, remembering what is one of the primary functions toward our ability to talk would definitely help increase our breathing conditioning.

If we were to really use our breathing before, during, and after talking, just think of some of the things that would have been said or not said. How many times I've reflected on what I've said. "If I only had taken a breath and thought one more moment, so much could have been avoided."

The next time you hear someone talking nonstop, or too loudly, or too anything, you might consider taking advantage of the apparent adversity, and *BREATHE.*

Believe it or not, some of the most valuable words I've spoken were to remind a person to breathe, or even to ask if they would like to. One of my favorite all-time buttons reads: "Create Miracles . . . Breathe!"

So Breathe It.

March 18
BREATHING FOR STRETCHING

I'm often asked how long one should stretch or hold a stretch for. The truth is, there's no one right answer. However, I believe there's a general way to stretch that holds true even for yoga stretches and postures.

There are very few "always do" things in life, but there is one in the world of stretching that comes close: "always" breathe out or exhale into any and all postures and stretches. In my opinion, the bare minimum is three full breaths, with a strong suggestion to hold a stretch for approximately five or more breaths. If translated into time, it ends up being at least 15 to 30 seconds. Of course in most yoga classes the instructor will hold postures for about 30 seconds to a minute.

In essence, if you can't relax and exhale during a stretch, you'd be wise to lessen the range of stretching. Remember, the value in a stretch comes with the relaxation of muscles, mind, and breathing.

Muscles are much like children. When the one in charge is peaceful, relaxed, and confident, the guided ones tend to respond in kind.

So Breathe It.

March 19
TWELVE-PRINCIPLE YOUR BREATHING

In Part 1 of *Wellativity: In-Powering Wellness Through Communication* we talked about *In-Powering* or *twelve-stepping* a person. Now I'd like to add to your breathing conditioning program by applying the twelve principles to increase your quality of breathing. We have done an inclusion of the twelve principles previously in another Daily Breath, but I think it would be extremely valuable to practice integrating your thinking with the principles and your breathing one more time.

Principle 1: Yes, my breathing is impaired.
Principle 2: I have help from the God within.
Principle 3: I choose to allow God to restore my breathing.
Principle 4: What I've recently done has made my breathing difficult.
Principle 5: "God, I know You know, but I need to say it to You."
Principle 6: "I'm ready and willing to have You restore my breathing."
Principle 7: "I humbly ask You to restore my breathing."
Principle 8: My past inhibited my breathing, but I'm willing to correct it.
Principle 9: This action is mine to safely take in my healing.
Principle 10: I continue to question if I'm breathing well.
Principle 11: I now practice my conscious breathing.
Principle 12: Practicing this is my example, and that helps the world.

So Breathe It.

March 20
EXTREME TEMPERATURE

All of us have experienced how difficult it can be to breathe when it's very hot or very cold. When we find ourselves in one of those extreme situations, it's a given that breathing will become more of a chore than we're comfortable with. Covering our mouths and noses with scarves, panting, or taking shorter breaths are all ways we find to sustain a consistent air flow. Next time you are in one of those extreme environments, after you've safely adjusted your breathing, I recommend you take the opportunity to consciously come to a place of gratitude for the usually moderate climates we're not only accustomed to but have been given by a benevolent God to live and breathe in.

How very fragile and vulnerable we are. I think we tend to forget the narrow comfort zone we all have until it's threatened. In science, the narrow acceptable environment for life to flourish is called "the goldilocks zone." Thank You, Creator of this land we live and breathe in. I'll rest here, because this place is just right. Amen.

So Breathe It.

March 21
EATING

I remember as a boy listening to my older brother eat. He would make grunting sounds that would usually make my father yell: "Mitchell, stop making so much noise when you eat!" Looking back, I now realize that Mitchell must have been barely breathing in order to make the sounds I recall.

As an adult I often notice that when I'm eating very fast I've held my breath for several bites of food. Although it's not easy for me, I do my best toward slowing down by putting my utensil down and taking a full breath or two before resuming. It's a fabulous habit to get into, not only for optimal digestion and enjoyment but also because it's said that eating slower helps to fill you up with less food, which in turn helps in weight management.

You might also remember that while eating when congested, you are not able to taste the food in the same way due to the limited breathing through your nose. The same holds true when eating very fast.

Help me to help myself eat at a healthy pace.
Help me when helping myself to another portion, to think and breathe.
Thank You, for this gift of breathing even helps me enjoy one of life's greatest pleasures, food.
Amen.

So Breathe It.

March 22
RUSHING

Nobody is a stranger to rushing once in a while, or should I say more than we like to admit. Obviously, rushing entails a degree of tension. In this experience, usually the first thing to be impaired is our breathing. If you think rationally about rushing or the need to move at a rapid pace, you would be aware that breathing or oxygenating our system would promote a higher quality of rapid movement.

Even if it's a flight or fight response, through reconditioning we can train ourselves to breathe well even in the most hurried moments.

Part of the reconditioning or reprogramming starts with the suggestion gained through reading these words. Then one time when you're rushing, the real win will be when you either remember this reading and/or just automatically adjust your breathing as you continue to move quickly.

There's nothing fundamentally unhealthy or unenlightened about rushing. It's what gets dropped out or included that makes all the difference. Safety first, breathe, yes I can accomplish this, faster, breathe, God is with me, don't forget that, breathe.

So Breathe It.

March 23
ENTERTAINMENT

It amazes me how much entertainment is geared toward "taking your breath away." We all know what an appetite our society has for watching violence, special effects, sex, mystery, horror, killing—during all of which we've found ourselves holding our breath for staggering amounts of time. Even if I have my own opinion of what's healthy or unhealthy viewing material, all of it can trigger us to breathe, rather than freeze. That's right, I've been conditioning myself to respond to shock and awe by breathing. Moreover, I even find anxiety or fear-producing scenes helpful. They assist me in identifying with what's real and unflappable within me. Being a long-time truth/ metaphysics/spirituality student, at this point I find it difficult to enjoy a horror movie as a regular viewer might. That being said, I still get tremendous value out of whatever show I'm watching.

The truth is, those people are actors doing their job very well, well enough to have me feel fear. Breathe, Scott. God is in charge, even in Hollywood. Amen.

So Breathe It.

March 24
BREATHEMAN

I've found that one of the pathways to the fountain of youth may be a childlike, creative faith or belief in the unseen. It's apparent to us as adults that we all too often have grown too intelligent for our own good. Please, consider the following as a "youthing" exercise.

What if you were to believe that there was a very real spirit speaking to you through the words you are reading? That the information given to you with respect to the 12 Principles and the Breathing Conditioning Program was at least in part brought to you by a common friend. His name, BreatheMan! With all the superhero attributes you so desire. He lives in the spirit world, so he's not confined to our earthly limitations.

Every time you remember to breathe, he's whispering to you.
When you drop your shoulders and stretch with a good breath, he's nudging you.
As you help others to do similar healthy things, BreatheMan is working with and through you.

So Breathe It.

March 25
RUNNING/JOGGING

Because my specialization as a health professional is joint replacement rehabilitation for hips and knees, in all honesty I can't recommend running as a completely safe form of aerobic exercise. However, within the bounds of moderation, I've personally found it to be one of the most conducive exercises for breathing conditioning. If you are one who insists on this form of working out, I'd like to mention a few things that could help.

First, keep your chest up to enable full breathing and spinal safety. Second, do your best to have less impact on your feet, which means limiting the height in which you leave the ground in your stride. Third, running for shorter distances with more intensity means less wear and tear on all of your joints. Finally, doing some conscious breathing exercises during your run is time and energy well spent during your journey. Once we've found something as exhilarating as running, balance, moderation, and integrity become the cornerstones of our safety.

Run as the Power Within you; may your path lead to good health and lasting peace. Amen.

So Breathe It.

March 26
LOVE

What if in your next breath you opened to a new understanding of love? As you breathe in, let the thought of love into your mind and body. As you breathe out, let go of all the misgivings you might have about love. What is love to you when you take away the judgments and evaluations of what it is? As you continue to gently breathe, consider letting the belief go that love involves romance, sex, giving to others, getting something, etc. What if love just were the very fabric of what we're all made of? Can you breathe in that possibility? It requires nothing. It wants nothing from you. It always has been and always will be.

It's OK to see love as we see it. But the question stands: are we putting limitations on what love is?

Just when I think I know what love is, then it shows me it's bigger than I had thought. Then I breathe a sigh. Why must I think I understand what love is? Do I fear something so beyond my mortal conception? Then again, I breathe. As a parent would comfort a child, I feel God letting me know it's OK. Then yes, I breathe in His love.

So Breathe It.

March 27
SUFFERING

There's no denying that so much of our human family is suffering. This fact I reluctantly breathe in. With this truth, I also breathe in the energy of hope and faith. I vow to hold this torch of belief for the ones who need time and space to come home to the truth.

When I relax and breathe, I let others know it's OK to do the same. We don't need to find our power. When we remember that we are powerful, we regain the privileges inherent within the Power.

At times we can feel guilt and shame that others will not walk in the light with us, but their suffering will pass when they are ready and willing to let go. My example is all I really have to give them.

A new day will dawn for those who stand strong.
When I see suffering, I breathe and pray.
It was once said that we could move mountains if we only had faith.
I just know that in the end, we will all live in peace.
Thank You, God, for keeping our eternal home safe and sound. Amen.

So Breathe It.

March 28
I AM WHAT I AM

I *have a body*, I am not my body. Every inch of it breathes for its life. I *have a brain* that thinks and is included as part of my body. And thus my brain breathes as well. For all that *I have*, I am grateful.

I am my Soul. I believe it breathes, too. The question I ask is "what exactly does it breathe?" I have a logical answer.

As my body breathes, to a large extent, what it's mostly made of—water/oxygen/hydrogen/carbon—so too my soul, I assume, does the same. The answer is God. In the eternal moment, in all logic and continuity, my soul must breathe in what it's made of—God. This is what was meant by saying, "Be still and know that I am God." As the wave moves and has its existence as an inseparable expression of the ocean, so too am I of God.

Be still, breathe, and know we are of God, every one of us.

So Breathe It.

March 29
NO MATTER WHAT

(Please breathe with each sentence.)

No matter what, everything is easier when we breathe.
Whatever the matter at hand, it's better dealt with when
we breathe.
What is, is, so just breathe with ease.
Nothing matters so much that it should stop us from
breathing.
As a matter of fact, breathing works in every situation.
Slowing down can be a matter of life and breath.
In order to have mind over matter, you will need to
breathe.
What's the matter? Take a breath, and remember this
too shall pass.
In the matter of you vs. the world, the verdict is . . .
breathe.
Does it really matter? Yes, no, maybe. So breathe
anyway.

*Sometimes I wonder if any of this really matters. Then I
remember, do my best, breathe, and leave the rest.*

So Breathe It.

March 30
SHARING

There's a popular saying which I've previously quoted: "you can't keep it unless you give it away." With regard to health and well-being, if we want to enhance something that works for us, sharing it with others/speaking it will make it more real and effective. For instance, if we suggest someone take a few breaths in order to relax or gain more focus, it's a given that we too shall do the same with them.

The truth about writing *Wellativity's Daily Breath* was that if it helped one person breathe, live, and be healthier, my goal would be accomplished. Between writing, and rereading, all of these Daily Breaths, I have proven that this simple conditioning process works! Take this book in any form you choose and let God's messages, and mine, transform you from within; remember, the more you share it with others, the more it will become real for you.

To give and receive are one in truth. What goes around comes around. Do unto others as you would have them do unto you—these statements basically have the same meaning. I pray that the light and love of God surrounds and enfolds you forevermore. Amen.

So Breathe It.

March 31
CONFUSION IS A HIGH STATE

I don't know many other conditions such as confusion that call on most of my spiritual attributes to maintain Peace. Asking God for help, trying to relax with a deep breath—take your pick. Or maybe it's more like walking through a house of mirrors in an amusement park. Either way, it's intense, and having an effective breathing habit will always prove advantageous.

There have been many moments in my life when my breathing was the only thing I knew for sure. It was the only thing that gave me an anchor into the here and now. Literally, my thoughts were, I'm still breathing, so I must be OK. Yes, the fact that I'm aware of my breath proves I am still alive. It must be that I've been granted another few moments of life, if only because I'm still able to breathe.

To be aware is to be alive. For this gift of consciousness, I give thanks.

So Breathe It.

April 1
BEING AN EXPERT

I've been told that if someone could be good at just one or two things in life, it would be a blessing or a gift from God. I've noticed that in the things I've come to be good or proficient at, there always comes a point when my mind and body are working together more than against each other. Maybe this ability of synchronistic being is foundational in "being an expert."

Once again, breathing definitely will have an active role in our demonstration of expertise or lack thereof. Isn't it amazing how this God-given function always shows up on so many levels in every moment? Here's the question of the day: what would it take for us to say we were an expert at breathing?

I know nothing, yet I trust myself completely. In this paradox, I breathe, let go, and just be, the best.

So Breathe It.

April 2
POST BREATHING

This reading has the theme of breathing after exercise. However, you can fill in the physical activity that is applicable for you.

I was sitting on a bench in the locker room after a solid workout session. It occurred to me that I was fatigued to the point that my breathing was taking more effort than was comfortable. I chose to close my eyes for a few moments and focus on deepening my breath. I then tried a new technique. Rather than try to force more air into my lungs, I attempted to push smaller amounts out and in turn let the vacuum happen in my lungs when air is pushed out. It worked, with much less effort than trying to force air in by muscular contraction. I recommend you try it for yourself.

Sometimes solutions come when we completely reverse our perception of how things have worked in the past.

So Breathe It.

April 3
EXERCISE THEMES: CRUNCHES

It can't be overemphasized how important it is to completely exhale when doing an abdominal crunch exercise as you contract your abdominals during the upward motion of your upper torso. The goal is to end up with no more air left in your lungs to push out. Then you hold for a moment or two with your shoulder blades raised off the floor.

Slowly letting your shoulder blades come back to the floor, you then allow the air to come back into your lungs for about a two count. This movement should be done slowly enough so that you begin your exhale/next upward crunch without resting just as your blades touch the floor. This technique is not only sound breathing for a standard crunch, but it goes far toward synchronizing your mind and body with your breathing; this in turn supports your overall breathing conditioning program.

The process of conditioning of our minds, bodies, and spirits involves a never-ending choice to start or focus on one or the other first. But will always involve our breathing regardless of the order.

So Breathe It.

April 4
WHAT'S YOUR SIGN?

Everyone receives different forms of communications guiding them in many directions. With regard to breathing, I find my reminders, or "signs" can be identical from one day to another but are also displaying themselves as ever-changing as well. For example, if I am exercising and see a person holding his or her breath, that almost always does the trick to reminding me to breathe immediately.

Sometimes I take an apparent negative like seeing someone smoking a cigarette, and I have the positive thought, "thank God for my free and easy breathing."

One of the major benefits to participating in your breathing conditioning program is ease and frequency. The reminders and signs that bring your awareness back to respiration take less and less effort as time goes by. In addition, more people and things will help you maintain a higher consciousness with respect to the importance of this subject for all of us.

Thank You, God, for Your unending supply of guides, teachers, and signs. Today I vow to look, listen, and respond in a new and improved way. Amen.

So Breathe It.

April 5
THE BUSINESS OF BREATHING

A simple and brief definition of what a business does is that it provides products or services for an equal return of payment in any number of forms. In this context, isn't breathing a business? Let's look at the product, the service, and the payment involved.

The product is oxygen or air provided for our bodies. The service is the action or act of inhaling and exhaling. The payment is renewed and sustained life to our bodies. We are the customers who have little or no choice about our patronage. Much like most of our electricity needs and patronages, the provider is not so much in question. The common ground is that breathing and electrical needs are not considered luxuries, but necessities. Like the energy companies, we too need the product and services provided by our company of air and oxygen supply. Our choice is the quality and quantity of our product we supply to ourselves.

Gratitude is the law of supply. My thank-you to the Universe/my God, is my continued patronage of Your product of oxygen.

So Breathe It.

April 6
BITTERSWEET PAST

No matter what our feelings are, it's always recommended to breathe into and through them, especially if they're intense to the point of being overwhelming. This is not to say that breathing should distract us from feeling what we are feeling, but healthy breathing habits will support every level of our well-being.

Our tendency is to contract our muscles during unpleasant or painful feelings. It would be wise to align our thoughts with our breathing in an expansive way. This is how it may look or sound during an intense experience:

Breathe, yes breathe as you feel the tightness in your throat as the sadness comes up. Try your best to relax the muscles in your neck, shoulders, and chest area. Breathe; whether you are feeling grief, anger, fear, or any combination, do your best to keep the flow of oxygen consistent without being taken away from what your feelings are telling you.

So Breathe It.

April 7
BEING DIFFERENT

The experience of feeling different or separate from people can bring forth many emotions. Having been disabled and orphaned as a young person, I completely empathize with loneliness, separation and isolation. Sometimes these feelings can run so deep that our breathing is the only friend we believe we have. So for a time, this may be our given reality. The ultimate reality is that our breathing was designed and given to us by our truest friend, God.

When I feel separate or oddly different from the world, I breathe knowing *everyone* breathes with me. *Everyone* needs to breathe right now in order to oxygenate their blood, which for all intents and purposes is the same for *everyone.*

God, we've all been woven from Your fabric, for which we thank You. For each fiber of your fabric that You eternally breathe life into, we all thank You. For the comfort that comes from knowing we are all connected in your unending thread of creation, we all extend our deepest gratitude. Amen

So Breathe It.

April 8
DIZZINESS

From time to time we all experience dizziness. In those moments conscious breathing could very well save our life, because dizziness will often lead to a state of panic. Regardless of how real and justified our fear might be, becoming unnecessarily tense will more often than not quickly make things worse.

Imagine a boat tied to a dock during a storm, in rough and choppy waters. Now picture the boat and the dock with rubberized buoys to cushion any contact. The buoys may not prevent severe damage, but they do help lessen the effects of most contact. In my opinion, this is what breathing can initially do for our bodies when they make inevitable contact with rough and choppy situations in life.

If you're alive today you've survived all the storms that life has presented in and around you. Breathe into the turbulence, the rough going, and the storm of emotions. Why? Because we know breathing works!

So Breathe It.

April 9
EXERCISE THEME: LEG LIFTS

With any weight-bearing movement in which pressure is placed on or around our backs, breathing and its sequence is critical. Of all the abdominal exercises, leg lifts put perhaps the most pressure on the lower back. The bottom line is that when we fully inhale, we create a stabilizing internal pressure on the lower back. So when we initiate the lifting of our legs a full inhale will help to protect the lower back area.

A slow 2-count movement as a basic protocol is safest. If you're confused about how or when to breathe, it's recommended with all exercises to take continuous breaths, trying to coordinate the inhales and exhales with different movements.

There is no one correct way of aligning our breathing with movement. However, some ways are definitely more effective and safer than others.

So Breathe It.

April 10
INTENSIVE CARE UNIT

Being in the ICU will bring anyone to a place of what it means to be in the moment. Honestly, I find it to be one of the most spiritual of experiences. When a person who is important to me was recently in the ICU, I was able to get a new appreciation for my life and my breathing. Every time I heard the respirator pump oxygen into my friend, I took it as an opportunity to consciously breathe with him. The interesting thing was that this action also brought me mentally and spiritually closer to him and to God. I'm not sure why, but something about consciously breathing together was like the three of us praying together for healing. It is in sync with the scripture: "Where two or more are gathered in my name [Jesus'], I am there among them."

Thank You, God, for all of the technology You have enabled us to develop and use for Your Will to be done on Earth. Amen.

So Breathe It.

April 11
IT'S NOT MY JOB

When working in the health profession it can be easy to think you can fix, heal, and help individuals who are not open or able to receive what's being offered. For a professional (or even a non-professional), it is most frustrating to know what will work toward a person's health and well-being and then have him or her be closed or shut down to what would appear to be best. Many times I've found myself taking a deep breath and sighing in a powerless exhale.

Sometimes the most profound things come at the most unexpected times. For instance, I was sitting in a therapy group and a person who was frustrated that a friend was not open to his much needed help blurted out: "God! he's your creation, YOU FIX HIM! IT'S NOT MY JOB!" Not the most prophetic statement, but for me at the time, it was as profound as it gets.

God, in these next few breaths, grant me the ability to trust that all is in Divine order; I may not be needed to do anything at the moment. Amen.

So Breathe It.

April 12
IN YOUR WAY

How common is the experience of someone being in our way when we'd prefer to maintain a certain speed of movement. Whether it be in a car, on a sidewalk, or on an escalator, it doesn't matter. It's all the same when another person impedes our intention. In these moments I would bet the farm that taking a few conscious breaths couldn't hurt, and it probably would even be the smartest thing we could do. This doesn't mean inaction or submission, but it is implying that a few grounding breaths will almost always help to reduce the intensity of your next decisions.

Going with God speed may mean fast, slow, stopped, or even backward. When we're in the inappropriate gear, our body/engine lets us know. Breathing is the clutch in the transmission to God speed.

So Breathe It.

April 13
WAITING FOR THE NEWS

There are not many things that can be more stress-producing than waiting for the news about someone's well-being. Maintaining an enlightened health-conscious attitude in a potential crisis will stretch our skills to the limit. All the visualizations, affirmations, and prayers are fine and good, but in the end, we come to a point of taking a big breath as we turn over the situation. "Thy Will be done" is much easier said when we're talking about someone else's loved ones. When it's about the one or ones we love and care for, being told to "trust the process" or that "all is in Divine order" can push us into having to take several deep breaths.

I like to think that the energy I am giving out will support a positive outcome for all involved. If I'm going to have fear-based thoughts, I'll double my efforts to not give in to holding tension throughout my body; the best way to do this is through conscious breathing and stretching.

We may be powerless over people, places, and things, but holding our breath and tensing our bodies will never change an outcome for the better. Just keep practicing expansive breathing. That will always help you to cope with all outcomes.

So Breathe It.

April 14
INCLUSION

Inclusion, or the act of including, is in direct opposition to excluding, or being separated from. Inclusion of people and their differences is not only one of the highest spiritual qualities one can have, but the lack of it is at the heart of humanity's deepest problems. I do my best to breathe deep when I see whole races of people excluding themselves as better than others. Certain religious sects, terrorist cells, and cults are just some of the extreme examples of what the opposite of inclusion is.

We are one race of humans, created by our Creator. When I see people nonjudgmentally including one another, I breathe easier. That doesn't mean sacrificing morals and values, but it does mean allowing all of us to have the space to be different without needing to convert in order to breathe comfortably.

What is so different between you and me that we can't celebrate our differences, rather than push each other away? So I breathe in my wish to have a world of inclusion, just as our Creator includes you, me, and everyone as His own.

So Breathe It.

April 15
INFLATABLES

I'm sure we've all gotten a bit dizzy blowing up some kind of inflatable at one point or another. This happens as the result of hyperventilation. The only way around this is to slow down. Usually a 5-count breath will be sufficient enough to maintain your equilibrium.

Looking at the muscle-strengthening dimension, manually inflating devices is excellent for your abdominals, your diaphragm, and your lung capacity. Next time you are thinking about using a pump to assist you in filling up items that require inflation, you might consider not bypassing the value of a little extra time and effort. Remember, there are many breathing exercises that will enable you to have increased oxygen intake on a long-term basis. Let's not let this one pass by.

There is usually more intrinsic value in just about every activity than initially appears to be. A few genuine moments of breathing and reflection will often yield a new perception that in turn opens a new level of value.

So Breathe It.

April 16
NONSTOP CHATTER

I was listening to one of my friends talk, and talk, and talk and wondering if she was actually breathing between sentences. No, really, I was wondering if she was breathing after every third or fourth sentence. It's funny, though, it could have made me more tense to listen and watch, but it seemed to have the opposite effect. It made me so appreciate each and every relaxed breath I was able to have as I nodded in agreement with what she was saying.

In all honesty, listening to someone's outer chatter is nearly as oppressive as listening to my own inner chattering of the nonstop conversation going 24/7. I guess my point is that when we find someone's chatter boring, maybe it's an opportunity to connect within ourselves to do a breathing check or a check of our body to see if we're holding any unwanted tension, or even an opportunity just to say a prayer.

The Universe is always speaking to us. That is, God always has something to share with us. The question is: are we listening from the right place?

So Breathe It.

April 17
EXERCISE THEME: SQUATS

It's suggested here, as with all exercise themes, that you consult a health professional with regard to your physical condition before beginning these exercises.

As indicated with the leg lifts, using an inhale to stabilize your lower back applies to doing squats or any other leg press or sitting actions. That being said, three things happen simultaneously. Breathing in, your backside going backward (to keep proper posture), and the squatting motion. By the time you've done a slow 2 count downward, your inhale and squat should be paused. Making sure your hips never go below your knees, hold for a 2 count and then begin slowly exhaling as you begin to stand up at a 2-count pace.

If you feel unstable doing this movement, using a chair, bench, couch, or person for support can help you until you feel more confident. It might be helpful to remember just how many times a day we all do the squatting motion. Every time we sit down on a chair, car, couch, toilet, at a desk, or on a train, bus, or plane, not to mention going up stairs, we are using the upward standing motion.

As with most tools given to us, breathing has an infinite number of mental, physical, and spiritual applications.

So Breathe It.

April 18
WASHING YOUR HANDS

Many years ago I read an extremely valuable book called *Zen Mind Beginners Mind*. One of the most important things I got from the book was that no act is more potentially spiritual than any other. To me that meant that whether it be washing my hands, painting a picture, or walking in the park, all in essence had the same spirituality involved. Thus it was up to the individual to consciously connect with their spirituality, in every act, to the best of their abilities.

The fact is that the Zen teachings show us that washing our hands can bring us as close to our spiritual nature as any High Holiday ritual performed. Thus, it is *all in where we come from*, or the context of our being in any and all actions. Wow! So the next time you wash your hands, it's up to you to do the rituals that bring your mind, body, and spirit into the act. For me it almost always starts with a conscious breath, and then maybe another.

If God is Omnipresent in all points of time and space, then what activity can we possibly say is more "Godly" than another?

So Breathe It!

April 19
LOWERING YOUR HEART RATE

It's now a proven fact that we can not only lower our heart rates but positively affect our entire body by learning to consciously relax our minds and bodies. Another obvious fact is that what we practice consistently, we get better at.

It may not be the goal of *Wellativity's Daily Breath* to lower our heart rates as well as to bring the other benefits that come from consciously breathing, praying, and affirming life through the readings. But if done on a regular basis, consciously relaxing our minds and bodies will certainly have an overall positive affect on our health and well-being.

Remember, Wellativity says that *communication is the primary means of optimizing our health.* This means the communications with ourselves, our bodies, our support network, and God. One of *Wellativity's Daily Breath*'s primary functions is to practice all of these forms of communication.

Yes, have a relaxed focus on something that brings peace to you.
And, believe that two things indeed work: Prayer and Breathing.

So Breathe It.

April 20
EXERCISE THEME: THE CHAIR

Many people are limited to exercising in a sitting position. The basics are the same for all. Wellativity endorses slow, isometric movements, which in the end minimize wear on all of the joints involved.

For this series of movements, extend your lower legs off the ground about 6 inches, with your hands and arms raised comfortably above your shoulders. Hold for a 2-3 count and slowly return your feet to the floor while gently and consistently breathing. Repeat this 8-10 times.

Now point your hands and arms directly out to the sides from your shoulders; while sitting, flex your lower leg as if you were standing on your tippy toes. Hold for a 2-3 count and slowly return while gently and consistently breathing. Repeat this 8-10 times.

These exercises are for anyone who is fit and medically able. Whether you're at your desk, in a parked car, or on a couch, these will benefit your body, your mind, and your breathing.

Even the simplest exercises can return you to the joy of movement. Breathe, hold, release, breathe.

So Breathe It.

April 21
SPINAL POSTURE

From my childhood days of hearing my father tell me to sit up straight, to my now adult years as a health professional when I'm hearing myself preach about the importance of spinal posture, it has been my whole life learning of this critical necessity toward our health.

In the context of breathing, when our spine is abnormally curved it will affect at the very least the depth of our oxygen intake capacity. Moreover, when our vertebrae are tilted or pinching excessively in any direction, our nerves can be adversely affected as well. As most of us know impaired nerves will make normal functioning of our organs almost impossible.

If you're not already working with back-strengthening exercises, I recommend first consulting an appropriate and trusted health professional. Second, when consciously breathing, gently lift your chest/upper torso to a comfortably erect posture. Remember, consistent, persistent, and long-term small efforts will lead to a substantial healthy difference.

In all dimensions we hold a "posture." Let's ask ourselves: What is my spiritual posture, right now? In your next few relaxed breaths, let your spirit not only show you but gently guide you to a loftier posture, or perspective of life. The thought that your Higher Power supports you, just as your spine helps your physical functions, can provide spiritual strength and flexibility.

So Breathe It.

April 22
WHAT'S IN THE MOMENT

The question of what's in the moment is loaded with more unanswerable questions than anything else. A Zen Buddhist might respond "everything/nothing is in the one eternal moment." For most of us however, that's a bit too esoteric. I can answer that question for myself at this moment: I'm on the train commuting into NYC as I'm writing this *Daily Breath* on my iPad. Right at this very moment, I'm taking a deep breath looking out at the Hudson River on a warm summer morning. I'm feeling a lot of feelings, and I'm doing my best to breathe into and through them. Now I'm having a thought of God and how He's inspiring me to write these words in a way that I hope will make a difference in someone's day as they read them. That is what my moment is right now. As I breathe now, I send these words off in a prayer of hope and service. Amen.

There truly is only one moment. Thus we can never really be anything but in the moment. Yes, our minds may drift through many universes, but don't we all eventually come back to be fully present? Whether it be now, or when we go into the beyond, we all have a choice in every moment.

So Breathe It.

April 23
SAYING NOTHING

This one I find personally quite challenging. There have been far more times when I've said something that I was to later regret than times when I'd said nothing. We'll probably never know what's best spoken, or not, in any given instance. But I know for sure that taking a moment or two to *think, breathe, and possibly pray,* will yield more peaceable results.

I breathe in the truth that words and silence well balanced are a good recipe for a God-centered outcome. As I see it, this is a lifetime practice of progress rather than perfection. When I've noticed I said something that did more harm than help, I breathe, and then put Principle 10 into action. I do this by taking safe and appropriate actions sooner rather than later.

God, I affirm that You are always there to guide my words and silence. Thank You for this ever-present support. I know You also send me messengers when I'm in need of more assistance. Amen.

So Breathe It.

April 24
MOST BREATHTAKING EXPERIENCES

The content of *the breathtaking experience* can of course be different for everyone. However, the training or conditioning around breathing remains the same for all.

For me, standing at the edge of the Grand Canyon was breathtaking to say the least. Looking down at my toes, which were inches from what I estimated to be an immediate 1000-foot drop, had me holding my breath. Stepping a couple of inches back, I was able to resume a regular breathing pattern. A smile came to my face when I saw a squirrel run in front of me as if to mock my uneasiness. He certainly had no breathing issues!

Considering the billions of years this planet has been evolving, in my opinion it's still dwarfed by what it must have taken to not only create but evolve humans to be who and what we are capable of. Just the fact that each of us has approximately 10 trillion cells, almost all of which breathe (have a degree of respiration) and abide by a divine plan, is awe inspiring.

The vast spaces we can see in the physical universe do not come close to the infinite space our minds can inhabit. In each breath we are enabled to create/witness more of the show.

So Breathe It.

April 25
GROUNDING

When we talk about "grounding" in electrical terms it's clear that we are referring to avoiding electrocution and/or fire. When we allude to the grounding of a person, the meaning can be more diverse.

For me, in essence to be grounded means maintaining a peaceful, sane, and compassionate perception of all that is. Yes, there are times and places for extreme feelings and experiences, but for the most part, breathing can be our grounding wire.

Laugh if you will, but there have been times when the experience of breathing was how I knew I was still alive in a body. By the same token, often by being aware of my continued breathing was how I concluded everything was OK.

Peace, sanity, and compassion may not be created by breathing, but our infinitely wise Creator has given us an anchor for each and every situation that may come upon us. Thank You, God, for the gift of breathing. Amen.

So Breathe It.

April 26
BREAKTHROUGH/BREAKDOWN

Call it the roller coaster of life, but I believe that there's a universal principal that involves the breaking through, winning, and/or reaching new achievements that inevitably bring us back to the state of breakdown, emotional low, and/or emptiness. Just about everything in creation is involved in a cycle.

The high of meeting a hard-earned goal can bring many exhilarated exhales of relief. Shortly after, though, we may be faced with holding our breath out of fear and confusion of what's to be next. Maybe to know that the accomplished individuals have mastered this inevitable cycle may help you to breathe easier. All I have to say now is, "breathe, the time for down-shifting will, as always, lead us to shifting back up to higher gears."

There is a season for all under the sun. Smiling, like breathing, helps the ones near you in ways beyond comprehension.

So Breathe It.

April 27
TO LOVE AND BE LOVED

Is there any more profound act of giving and receiving than to love? Like breathing, one must take it in in order to give back. If you are truly loving someone, you must have received love from a source. Whether it was from yourself, another person, or from God to be a conduit, it must follow the universal law of giving and receiving.

I breathe love into you. You breathe love into me. We breathe love into each other, together. We nourish our life by freely giving and receiving God's love. We breathe His air, eat His food, and are nurtured by His warmth. Like two branches of the same tree, we hold strong during the changing currents of life.

Together we enjoy the breathing, eating, and drinking of His sustenance. For of the sharing of His love, I'm sure He has no grander pleasure.

So Breathe It.

April 28
BEING ATTACKED

Justified or unjustified, we've all been attacked. In our outer world, not knowing the details, I can't really give any valid advice. However, dealing with adverse situations in our minds and bodies can be prepared for here.

There is nothing that will thrust us into a primal and instinctual reaction than being attacked. It would be unwise to tell you to stop and breathe if the best immediate advice would be to run or defend. That being said, once our safety is secured, our best advice is indeed to *BREATHE.* There's no more important time to bring oxygenated air into our system than when we are in a fight or flight mode. Let this message go with you in even the most apparently "unenlightened" or "nonspiritual" experiences.

Turning the other cheek, forgiving 70 times 70 times, or a stand of nonviolence does not preempt safety and being real given our subjective experience. I do, however, do my best at living by the value of "do unto others as I would have them do unto me." Getting back to my breathing can help me remember this.

So Breathe It.

April 29
FILL IN THE BLANK

This fill-in-the-blank *Daily Breath* is designed to fit any and all situations. Your job is to simply choose the word that best fits an experience this breathing conditioning program has not covered.

In this experience of _____ I shall breathe fully and completely. There's no situation that would not benefit me in quickly coming back to conscious breathing. _____ will be there or not, but my anchoring into my spirit through breathing can only lead to a better outcome for all.

God, I know You've put _____ in my path for the best of all involved. I can remember Your ultimate best intentions when I breathe my way back to the consciousness of Your undying love and presence. Even this fact I know You have woven into my design. Thank You for the evolutionary purpose of being able to freely choose. My prayer of gratitude back to You is: May our Wills be one. Amen.

So Breathe It.

April 30
HOLDING ON AND LETTING GO

I have yet to see a dimension in life that does not speak of the value of balance. With regard to the topic of holding on and letting go, it would surprise me to hear someone say "it's always beneficial to let go, relax, and trust." The closest I can get comfortable with this is, "let go of what's best to let go of and trust people, places, and things for what they're trustworthy of." Other than that, I'll take a breath, or two, and do my best to have a nonjudgmental, compassionate perception in any given situation.

I hold on to the belief that God goes with me always. "I breathe into the experience of letting go" of any unwarranted fears. In my next breath I hold strongly to the conviction of honesty, even when it's not comfortable; then I take a full breath once again as I let go of the past, knowing that it is over, and *it cannot hurt me.*

Dear God, help me to help myself in knowing when to stand strong and when to release what's best to let go of. I ask You also to help me to see beyond my ego, to a balanced, and real place of what's best for all concerned. Amen.

So Breathe It.

May 1
EXERCISE THEME: JOINT INTEGRITY

The health and maintenance (joint integrity) of the joints in our bodies is among the most important aspects to any fitness program. Unfortunately, this more often than not takes a back seat to new and different program design. I can't tell you how many times a day I must take a deep breath as I see more and more fitness programs disregard knees, lower backs, and shoulders (so often seen with Plyometrics and kettle bell training) in the pursuit of muscle tone and strength. Being in the health and fitness arena on a daily basis, my challenge is to put into practice Principle and Step One, dealing with being powerless and the unmanageability of what I see unfolding in my industry.

As discussed in previous exercise themes, slowing movement with weights and isometrics (stopping motion midway through a repetition to prevent momentum cheating) helps to cut down on the need for higher repetitions, which helps to reduce wear on your joints. In addition, slowing down weight-bearing movements contributes to the awareness of your breathing.

Any fitness program based primarily on physical appearance/ego is bound to bypass some of the long-term issues concerning safety and the integrity of your overall health and fitness.

So Breathe It.

May 2
ORDERING FOOD

It may sound a bit farfetched to say our breathing habits can help us achieve and maintain a healthy body weight. But if we look at just one example, that of being in a restaurant and contending with the onslaught of desires and temptations that appear on the menu, we must see that breathing can be our best line of defense. As for myself, there've been several occasions when I've reduced my caloric intake by hundreds due to the timely response of some last-second defensive breathing strategies. Would that not be classified as "breathing as weight management"?

If there can be an energy or dysfunctional force involved with and around food (and there's no doubt that for many of us there is), then according to all that *Wellativity's Daily Breath* stands for, conscious breathing in those pivotal moments can make all the difference. This is yet one more valid reason for regularly participating in your breathing conditioning program.

Not only are we all connected, but all of our challenges are as well. Now that we have learned when, where, and how to use our tools (primarily breathing), the challenge comes down to whether we remember to use them. In many of our 12-Step programs it is common knowledge that our afflictions often boil down to a dysfunction based in our memory, or a disease of forgetting.

So Breathe It.

May 3
BEING IN LOVE

Love can mean many things for each of us. I believe we can agree that it is one of the most intense energies or emotions we can experience. Wellativity defines love as the fabric or essence of which God/the Universe is made. So being romantically in love with someone can be seen as nothing standing between you, your loved one, and God. Given all that could intrude in this holy trinity, is it not wise to have healthy breathing habits intact while dealing with the roller coaster of coupling human love with the Divine?

Fear, jealousy, and possessiveness have all been known to interfere in order to separate us from the purity of true love. When I find myself caught in the web of fear-based feelings, I'm usually not having relaxed breathing. Rather than trying to get rid of my feelings, I'll do my best to include them as I focus on taking some healing breaths.

The more I acknowledge Your presence, God, the more fear and its offspring have difficulty taking root. This is in alignment with Your universal truth of "where there is light, darkness cannot exist." Amen.

So Breathe It.

May 4
CAUGHT IN THE MACHINERY

Being caught in the machinery here is about a state of consciousness. One, it's the misconception that any machine can function outside of the *divine order of God's universe,* and all the immutable laws of his/her physics. Second, it is a belief that the functioning of a machine, or the lack of it, can have any bearing with the connection to our source of life/God.

Let's say I'm sitting in an overheated car on the side of the road:

God, help me to forgive myself for thinking that prayer alone would compensate for my not tuning up this car when I knew it was time. Thank You, God, for the thought I'm having now to breathe. I forgive myself for ignoring the signs You gave me. It makes it easier to breathe, now that You've helped me remember that this too shall pass. Amen.

So Breathe It.

May 5
EGO DOWNSIZING

If I just look at my life alone, I see that it has definitely been a process, or a journey, of downsizing my ego. A child's point of view is that the world revolves around him and exists only to gratify each of his needs. My "downsizing" was not always an easy path of growing up. "It's all about my needs and what I want" doesn't just evaporate with my conscious breathing. However, when I become aware that I may be reverting to my egocentric ways, a few breaths can often yield the pause needed to determine what could be the next right thing to do in a situation.

The "I can go it alone" or the "my way is best" attitude usually can be helped by my conscious breathing to have a shot at not being so willful.

God, as I breathe with You, let our wills be one. Amen.

So Breathe It.

May 6
GOD OF MY UNDERSTANDING

Did you ever find yourself taking a deep breath followed by a loud sigh, because you just couldn't understand why certain people wouldn't allow you to see and believe in God, *as you understand Him/Her?* Clearly God is not forcing anyone to view His existence (or lack of it) in any one way. So why do many people find the need to force their beliefs on others, if there's no evidence that God has ever done that to anyone?

The God of my understanding is writing these very words through my hands. He knows how valuable *Wellativity's Daily Breath*'s conditioning program is. It's not to be pushed onto anyone. However, persistence and repetition are what I believe he wants us to understand are key. God designed every aspect of our breathing and also designed the freedom for us to choose to use our breathing toward all its infinite advantages.

Next time you have a conscious thought about breathing, realize that God knows exactly what you're thinking. Not only that, but He is the reason you have this book in your hands. The use of it, He knows, will demonstrate your level of growth.

So Breathe It.

May 7
WHAT'S LOVE GOT TO DO WITH IT?

In one word, *everything*. Giving all of us the benefit of the doubt, let's agree that love was present between your parents at your conception. Also considering the varying degrees of reaction one could have to this subject, I recommend you breathe at this point, regardless of your feelings toward your parents of origin.

In spirit, and in truth, I believe our parent of origin is our Creator. And if the essence of God is love, then it follows that our essence is that of love too. When addressing the issue of God, parents, and love we can't be reminded too often to breathe. It's a good bet that all of us have at least one or two emotion-packed issues in this area.

Love, trust, patience, faith, and strength are all within us. The earthly and/or human attributes of these qualities are as varied as the number of people living. On our gratitude lists, we might consider remembering that these Divine gifts can be accessed by taking a breath and becoming aware that they all are what we are made of.

So Breathe It.

May 8
THE BULL EXERCISE

When I was a teenager I had the privilege of participating in a therapeutic/self-transformational group that gave us many exercises toward our growth as a person. In one exercise I was instructed to sing a song in front of the group and do my best to move them to join me in singing. Until they were successfully persuaded, they were to say only "Bull&%!#" in reaction to my singing. The bottom line for me was to work through my feeling of rejection and fear until I could finally succeed. As you may understand, in the light of such verbal rejection, my breathing was my only friend for many moments.

Whether it be dating, being interviewed, or selling something, we will all have to deal with intense feelings of rejection, failure, and/or humiliation. During these growth experiences, grounding ourselves with the help of a Higher Power can save us a lot of hurt and pain. In the middle of the storm our Higher Power might just get its foot in the door of our consciousness with one breath of letting go.

Be still and know, our Higher Power is one with us. It knows what we have need of, and what we want. We've made it this far, could it be possible that all has been provided? Trust the process.

So Breathe It.

May 9
URBAN ETHICS: CITY SMOKERS

When entering any and all cities I would love to see posted their Urban Ethics. These would be agreed principles for peaceful and respectful coexistence. We would find them at all city entry points. Bridges, tunnels, toll booths, roadways, railways, airports, etc. You might be wondering what this has to do with breathing conditioning. Let's start with cigarette smoking and secondhand smoke. The posted ethic might state: "Please refrain from smoking in public areas where people are within approximately 15 feet of you at any given time." It will help them to breathe easier. This urban ethic would insist that smokers at least be conscious of what they're doing and know that it would affect others in less than healthy ways. We're not asking the smoker to do anything other than respect other people's lungs, especially when they have little or no choice to avoid the smoke. In other words, if you must smoke, please do so at your own risk, not that of others.

We live in a cause-and-effect universe. We make a difference. Do unto others as you would have them do unto you. What goes around, comes around. All of the principles, aspired to, would go far toward healing ourselves and the planet. Breathe, my friend; nothing is impossible.

So Breathe It.

May 10
SAFETY, SOBRIETY, AND SERENITY

When we look closely at each item in this topic, we see that it's near impossible to have only one of these qualities without having all of them. Without safety we definitely cannot be at peace or experience any real level of serenity. Without our rational, sane, and also known as sober thinking, our safety is certainly at risk; thus little or no serenity. Each is very much related and relative (wellative) to each other.

Let's breathe in the feeling of gratitude for our safety, sobriety, and serenity. And in turn our exhales can reflect all thoughts and feeling that could get in the way of these foundations to health and well-being.

"Thank You, God, for all that true health is built on." The cup that is made of safety, sobriety, and serenity is what I fill with Your love. All can be nourished from this vessel, as long as it is kept intact. Thank You, God, for my ability to serve and be served. Amen.

So Breathe It.

May 11
LOYALTY

Most people have a clear understanding of what it means to be loyal to a person or an organization. By definition, to be loyal is to show a strong support or allegiance. I'm sure there's no mistake with regard to the origin of the word, how loyalty and royalty not only sound alike, but can be closely related. If you did not show your loyalty to the King or the Queen, you might very well have been taking your final breaths of life.

For you, me, and the subject of The Daily Breath, showing your loyalty to God would be a more appropriate conversation here. Every time we say a prayer of gratitude, or affirm Gods Life within and around us, or turn our will and our lives over to the God of our understanding, we are demonstrating loyalty in its highest form.

Whether I bow, get on my knees, or look up to the sky, it doesn't matter quite as much as what I keep in my heart and soul. Let this message ring out loud and clear as a continued confirmation of our love and gratitude for You, God. We breathe in Your life substance and just say thank You for all You have freely given us. For with You stands our truest loyalty. Amen.

So Breathe It.

May 12
BREATHING YOUR HEART RATE DOWN

It's a scientific and medical fact that we can consciously lower our heart rates by what we think and do. In my training I was told to "go to the beach." I would see my inhales and exhales like the waves in the ocean I was visualizing, rolling in and then retreating back. Sure enough after a minute or two of doing that, my heart rate would be reduced by several beats per minute. When I exercise now I often do conscious breathing and watch my heart rate on the monitors. Stabilizing or even dropping down with my beats per minute (bpm) is often the result.

"To be aware is to be alive" is one of the philosophies of a well-known organization. To be alive, to me, means to be able to make conscious choices towards the quantity and quality of my life, as well as the lives of others. Whether it be our heart rate, our breathing, our behaviors, or our thoughts and words, awareness is the starting point of all safety and improvement.

Remember Wellativity's acronym of WAIT: What Am I Thinking, and Where Am I Tense? It's all about what's going on in and around us. No matter where, what, or when, also remember that BREATHING WORKS.

So Breathe It.

May 13
DON'T WALK

Walking through New York City on a daily basis, as I do, can challenge even the most enlightened people of the human race. Often it's rush here, go there, avoid getting bumped into and/or hit by moving vehicles. Pedestrians often need to stop at Don't Walk signals at least every few blocks. I take that opportunity to breathe, stretch, or even look up at the sky, which in turn helps me remember that there's more to this massive machine than just getting from one place to another.

Don't Walk signals are a golden opportunity to reconnect within and/or stretch our muscles. Curbs, lamp posts, and fire hydrants are just some of the items that can be used to enhance stretches. Of course putting safety first is paramount, but you may also consider closing your eyes for 5 or 10 seconds for a few conscious breaths. Why not try to come up with a couple of things that will help you to stay grounded and connected within as you travel through your world?

What is really meant when we hear a person say "Godspeed"? After I let go of my perception that it means "super fast," I get the understanding of "Thy Will be done." This could mean an indefinite holding pattern, or it could mean it's already happened. "In His time, not mine," works too.

So Breathe it.

May 14
HEALTH CLUB/GYM ETHICS

There is no better way to start a series on ethics of any kind than to base all that is said on the biblical statement "do unto others as you would have them do unto you." Therefore, let's consider that we all breathe and most of us are sensitive to odors. The health clubs being an environment where people are in close proximity, how we smell will rank among the top ethical things to talk about.

Obviously breathing, exercising, and odors are easily discussed together. From my experience of being in gyms first thing in the morning, it has become clear that many people don't consider that, bathing (or not), using excessive amounts of perfume or cologne, and/or brushing their teeth (or not) will affect how breathing is accomplished by persons near them. Aside from the bottom line of intrinsic value of thinking of our breathing here, if even one person remembers to help the club environment by considering how he will affect others, this *Daily Breath* has worked well.

What goes around comes around. Need more be said?

So Breathe It.

May 15
INNER SPACE

When the outer world is presenting a challenge for us, we sometimes find ourselves reaching for a peaceful place. Many have referred to this place as our inner sanctuary, a place of communion with a Higher Power, or even just our center. Every human being can have a different name for it. But in truth it's the same for everyone. It is a place no one else can enter. A place that is completely safe and easy to breathe in. A space of total peace and quiet.

It is the place where we connect with God. The only cost to entering this sacred place is our willingness to let go of the outer world. In our release is everyone's Peace.

So Breathe It.

May 16
TAKING THE GOOD WITH THE BAD

Isn't it amazing how we so often allow one "bad" thing to invalidate 10 "good" things? I find myself taking many deep breaths on behalf of accepting my own imperfections, as well as those of others. My rhetorical question is, at what point did we grow so intolerant of our imperfections? In reality, not one of us is qualified to ever, ever "cast the first stone," or "throw rocks at glass houses."

When I mess up, the first thing I do my best to do is to breathe. When you mess up, yes, I must first breathe too. Growth is messy, and none of us is finished growing up until God says so. Until then, I vow to do my best not to be so harsh when it comes to judging myself and others. So, on my inhale, I will say, *"EASY,"* and on my exhale, I whisper, *"DOES IT."*

God, help me to help myself, not to infect understanding and healing with my judgmental thinking. Amen.

So Breathe It.

May 17
CENTER VENTILATION

When we go to a temple, church, mosque, or any place we deem as holy ground, most of us go there to be spiritually revitalized. Affirming our truth, as we understand it, is breathing to our spirit. Just as our bodies need to breathe oxygen, so our spirits need to breathe for life; just as our air is made of a few basic elements, so is spiritual life composed of basic elements. I believe they are love and truth.

Each of us has a different lung capacity. Too much or too little air is detrimental to us. Is it not the same for our minds and spirits? An excess, or scarcity, of truth and love can be too much for us to handle.

Our center, or where our soul lives, needs maintaining as does a church or temple in the world. When we physically breathe, let's remember to spiritually and mentally breathe with our thoughts and feelings.

So Breathe It.

May 18
THINK, THINK, THINK

One of the most popular signs in the 12-Step rooms throughout the country (and probably the world), is the "Think" saying. It's printed three times, one on top of each other, and almost always is hung upside down. Wellativity's WAIT acronym of "What Am I Thinking?" could be closely related to "Think." *Wellativity's Daily Breath's* version would clearly be "Breathe, Breathe, Breathe." However, I would place the word "breathe" in three different directions. This would imply breathing in any condition, direction, and place.

Once our breathing conditioning is in a place where we can say "my breathing has drastically improved," and our signs and signals to check our breathing are regular and consistent, we can enjoy being alive in a different way, just as when we've gone through the difficult initial stages of building a habit of exercise, we then can also enjoy a different way of having and being in a fit body. Some of the physical improvements from better breathing habits may be: fewer headaches, less muscular tension, clearer thinking, more energy, and less adverse effects from stress.

Breathe, ehtaerb, BREATHE.

So Breathe It.

May 19
THE BURNING ASH

I remember once reading in a spiritual enlightenment book about how a master taught his students to deal with negative thinking. He said one should deal with negative thinking as if it were a burning ash on your sleeve. Without a second thought, you would flick the burning ember with you finger before it could cause any more damage. Going into denial about what needs to be the next right decision for us is not the point. It's taking immediate action with regard to how we are thinking.

We notice a negative thought pattern, (flick it) the thought to pause and breathe. A moment to breathe almost always will enable us to think in a saner and sober way. This is a suggestion to practice. Nobody has perfected dealing with all "burning ash" situations. Not even the most enlightened beings we've heard of could say they've mastered the world of today. Sitting under a tree meditating can be an easy way to master being centered, but navigating through rush hour is totally different.

Practice makes progress, not perfection.

So Breathe It.

May 20
THY WILL

The commonly known phrase *Thy Will be done, not mine,* is understood by most of us to mean God's Will be done, not our own smaller needs and wants. As you may have read previously, one of my "New-Age" adaptations to this is: *May our Wills be one.* To me, this accounts for our God-given design of complete choice, not just a surrendering of our will but a choice of partnership.

A further extension and transformation of a similar statement, *God Willing,* is my lifetime heartfelt prayer. However, to me, this somehow does not account for an evolved and mature partnering (or co-creating) of Wills. So the next time you're thinking of saying "God Willing such and such will happen," you might consider saying, "*All Willing* this will come to pass."

The breathing aligned affirmation/prayer is:

(inhale while saying) "May our Wills"
(then exhale saying) "be one."
Also: (inhale) "All Willing"
(exhale) "it will happen."

So Breathe It.

May 21
CHOPPING WOOD, CARRYING WATER

This is a phrase that was meant to refer to everyday mundane chores and activities. The implications of Zen Buddhism and eastern philosophy are intended here. In other words, *just* chopping wood or *just* carrying water puts an emphasis on doing only the task at hand. No other mental, emotional, or physical activities are to intrude into the enjoyment of simply chopping wood and carrying water.

When I notice how many things are going on inside my head, not to mention my feelings, during a simple task, I first remind myself to breathe. Then as nonjudgmentally as possible, I acknowledge the things that are preventing my simply enjoying the task at hand, and then I consciously breathe again, and again.

It has been said: "Be here now, with nothing added."
Wellativity's Daily Breath says: "Breathe here now, with everything and/or nothing added."

So Breathe It.

May 22
THE LITTLE THINGS

Not letting the little things bother us may or may not be wise. Many times I've noticed that the little things tend to add up to big things. For me, when I turn over my life and each situation, big or little, to my Higher Power I can count on the support regardless of the magnitude of the situation. I can usually tell what I'm turning over by the depth of my following breaths. By the same token, I can tell whether I'm resisting giving my life and affairs over to the care of God by my breathing as well.

If I get cut off while driving, it's not a big deal if I'm safe and sound. Whatever it takes to quickly release the incident safely is what is needed. Ideally, I breathe, acknowledge my feelings and judgments, and breathe again. I must admit that between the first and last conscious breath, I sometimes let go with a loud expletive. Of course I write that off to releasing my upset, so as to not repress my feelings.

There is no concern too big or too small for the God of your understanding. From the creation of the Universe, to each atom, He/She/It lives within.

So Breathe It.

May 23
I'M IN TUNE

When our mind, body, and spirit are in tune, is it not as pleasant as experiencing a favorite song or symphony? We all have been given ample tools to "get and stay in tune." It clearly is a lifetime process for us all. For me, conscious breathing (as you might by this point have realized) is my first and foremost tool of connecting within. This means connecting with God, my spirit, and all that is compassionately benevolent.

When a musician picks up his or her instrument, it usually will take some tuning/adjusting for the chords to be in tune. For us, when we wake up or pick up our bodies from sleep, prayer, meditation, breathing, or affirming, we have the potential to start our day more in tune with what we see as most important. Once, twice, or a hundred times through the day may be what's needed to stay in tune.

There is a universal melody of life that is said to be eternally vibrating through all the Universe. If we get real quiet, it can be enjoyed by all of us.

So Breathe It.

May 24
BEING WITH IT

For me, one of life's greatest and most difficult lessons is the skill, or should I say art, of just being with my feelings. If I were given the choice to go back in time, I couldn't honestly say I'd feel right about changing any past situations or events because of the intrinsic value that goes far beyond my human understanding. However, what I would teach myself, or plead with the ones teaching me, is how to initially just be with things without acting from a place of hurt, anger, or sadness.

This is yet another gift that conscious breathing is able to assist us with. Even two or three quiet breaths can slow the torrent of emotions that usually do not benefit decision making. Even if we act impulsively it's not too late to slow down, breathe, and make healthy adjustments or amends (Wellativity's 10th Principle).

Breathing works! It also can help make time for the miracle of peaceful, sane, and loving action.

So Breathe It.

May 25
KEEPING MY HEAD UP WHILE I LOOK DOWN

No doubt we all have certain people, places, and things that we'd be wise to stay away from, let alone even look at for too long. Walking through New York City on almost a daily basis for well over 30 years, I've learned just how many opportunities there are to be triggered. That is by food, lustful pictures, ads for alcohol, violent media, and much more. So many deep breaths I've taken on just as many streets. The question for me has come down to where my deepest energies live. If I'm not willing to have my Higher Power transform me from within, then all the looking down or away is limited in its value.

There are many prayers for welcoming help, guidance, and healing. From my own experiences, I strongly recommend we all incorporate along with our conscious breathing a regimen of prayer and affirmation. Here is one that may work for you walking down the streets in your life.

God, I feel powerless over this need. As I breathe, I loosen my grip on this issue, so You may lift it away from me. I know You will not, until I have freely turned it over to You. Thank You, God, for Your help when You deem it is time to remove my shortcomings. My prayer is one of preparation. Preparing myself to the best of my ability for Your love and support, which is boundless. Amen.

So Breathe It.

May 26
ZEN OF PIN PLACEMENT

I've coined this term for when I'm working out in the gym. Many of the weightlifting machines have pins to adjust the pounds one lifts. This Zen term has come from me incorporating inner/spiritual connection with what my body is able to do. Mind you, there is no replacement for slowly learning through professional and systematic training. However, I did learn when my training was incorporated into my mind and body to the point at which I could release certain structure in my exercising.

As Wellativity's core principle states, health is primarily a function of communication; I bring this to a high level when exercising personally and professionally. For example: I walk up to a weight machine, close my eyes for a moment, and clear my mind of preconceived ideas of what I thought I could do. Then I breathe a few conscious breaths and let my hands put the pin at the inner guided weight. For me, this adds an incredible spiritual aspect to pumping iron.

God, Guides, Angels, and your Higher Power are with you always and in all ways. Have you learned not only to call upon them when you need help, but also to include them in the fun and joy of your movement? They most certainly will respond to the calling.

So Breathe It.

May 27
CREATE LIFE AS IT IS

Our perception of life is unique. Do you know what possibilities that implies? Not having lived this moment, this day, or the situation(s) you'll be in, you have the freedom to choose how and what to bring to the show. Take a second to breathe in this concept. Okay, God may be seen as the executive producer, but you are the actor or actress, director, the screen writer, and the producer! Create, or re-create your part as you see fit. If you've had a tough part so far, that's all the more reason to write in a heroic outcome.

Goethe once wrote that "boldness has genius...in it." I believe he meant that by making the commitment (boldness) to see things differently (using our creativity), we activate the genius within. In order to do this, we must start right where we are, not where we wish to be. In other words, the first scene we're in, we have to "create life as it is!"

God has already granted me the serenity to accept the way things are; the courage to change the things I choose to; the wisdom to know the difference. Amen.

So Breathe It.

May 28
NEED TO CONTROL

Nobody is foreign to the need to control things in life. Certain things definitely benefit from this need. However, many of us get into the habit of trying to control things that are not meant to be controlled by us. In the realm of recovery from afflictions, it's called "being powerless" over something. The common misconception is that by acknowledging our powerlessness, we have no choice. To the contrary, once we become honest with our given powerlessness, we then begin to know true Power.

Our Higher Power is there to guide us to and from things. If we insist on trying to defy our shortcomings, there's not much the Power can do for us. However, when we give up the fight, our egos no longer will have much success in running the show. This will possibly require us to breathe a few more conscious breaths. Giving up our need to control can be a bit scary though in the end we may find ourselves breathing easier.

Having faith and trust, especially in that which cannot be seen, is not always easy. Like the technology of our rapidly advancing society, God's promised faithfulness not only takes practice to use but trust that it will work. I believe that with practice and trust, much greater works are available to us, in and through Him who has given us life.

So Breathe It.

May 29
STEP BACK

In this context, stepping back implies taking a breath or two and hopefully buying a few moments to see things from a loftier perspective. Seeing things from the highest point of view takes tremendous spiritual grounding. It requires us to be willing to let go of limiting perceptions. Personally, I'm often limited by my fear, ego, and aggression, not to mention past experiences.

Taking time to breathe is critical so as to enable the wisdom and benevolence that lives within us to have its voice. It speaks to me in many ways: "Maybe that person wasn't aware of how his action would make you feel. She might be rushing to help someone in need. Have you not forgotten to consider how your behavior might affect others?" It's obvious when someone is being downright offensive, but if this offers us a chance to change our own thinking, it would serve us most of all.

Charitable thinking has some very healing properties. Most of these are for ourselves. To be charitable in our thoughts means to give a person the benefit of the doubt. It also means to see that person, like ourselves, as a work in progress.

So Breathe It.

May 30
BATHROOM BREAK

For many people the bathroom is one of the only opportunities to have peace and quiet, let alone solitude. Yes, it usually is a place of taking care of physical needs, but what if we reconsider bathroom time as more inclusive. That is, to include it in our consciousness as a time to reconnect within. Not only can conscious breathing help us to eliminate what we need to in a restroom, it's an opportunity to be grateful that your body is functioning as it does.

In addition, remember that God designed us to be able to freely eliminate, detoxify, and make room for more sustenance. A function that is so often quickly taken care of could easily be taken for granted. That is, unless we construct our consciousness to see the opportunity. Our breathing, our digestion, all of our functions, including our planet and solar system, are part of the huge cycle of life. To think of this can help us breathe a breath of amazement!

To give and to receive are one in truth.

So Breathe It.

May 31
CALORIE BURNING

For those who are concerned with weight reduction, it's a fact that better breathing habits lead to burning more calories. We know that when a muscle works it burns stored energy, or calories. Taking the concept further, the diaphragm (the muscle responsible for breathing) uses much less energy when the breath is shallow. By conditioning full regular breathing, the calories burned far exceed those used during subpar respiration. The diaphragm must pull itself substantially further down to take in more air; in addition it follows suit that pushing more used air out indeed burns more calories as well.

When you add exercise and occasional deep breathing (in which you completely inhale and exhale all the way out, this being a common yoga exercise to stretch the diaphragm), over a day, a week, and much more, the calories burned multiply into thousands. Hopefully this Daily Breath can give you some real and factual inspiration toward improving your respiration.

If there's one thing most every human is proficient at, it's gathering evidence or reasons for our actions. Knowing the benefits of better breathing habits can motivate us to keep on keeping on.

So Breathe It.

June 1
NON-RESISTANCE

If there were one quality I could say I'd like to have in most every situation, it would be that of non-resistance. I believe the main contributing factors to "resisting" or "resistance" are tension, conflict, and fear. Could there be anything that's more limiting to our breathing, let alone to our over-all health? An Eastern philosophy book I once read said when we pass on to the other side, we should do our best to remember one thing—non-resistance.

Aside from hurt and pain, I think we resist aging most. This is yet another reason to have healthy breathing habits. I think of aging, and I automatically breathe. What more than increasing our oxygen intake can we do in this moment to support our entire system? I breathe in and say "non," and breathe out saying, "resistance." If we breathe into the thoughts we most welcome rather than contract into the undesired ones, we'd be all the wiser.

What I resist shall persist. It is safe and natural to love and be loved. I was born to share God's love. Amen.

So Breathe It.

June 2
URBAN ETHICS: SIDESTEPPING

There is an unspoken protocol in which pedestrians stay to the right while walking toward another person. I tend to get physically defensive when someone is walking straight at me (often not paying attention due to texting or talking). Breathing is effective for my inner well-being, but it often has to take a back seat to a quick maneuver. It's a funny thing, though: if I'm breathing, moving more consciously, and coming from a peaceful place, even the disruptions are more easily dealt with. Things even seem to happen at a more tolerable pace when I'm connected within.

By breathing, and stepping aside more often than insisting on my right of way, I am going easier on myself as well as the rest of the city. In the end, my righteousness is a very expensive indulgence. If my breathing is not enough to slow me down, I can always count on my Higher Power to put speed bumps along my way.

All is in Divine order. That includes me, everyone else, and the help that is sent to me. I may not see it always, but it's comforting to know I'm not running the show.

So Breathe It.

June 3
MASTERY OF WAITING

One of the wisest things I've ever heard was a sage talking about waiting. He said, "A person who has mastered waiting, has mastered life." At first I didn't understand the full implication. After a few contemplative thoughts, and breaths, it dawned on me just how accurate the man was. You might agree if you look at one of your own days. For instance, just within the first hour or two this morning, I've waited for my coffee, the shower to warm up, my computer to boot up, the weather report, the train to come, ideas for writing, and my arrival in NYC. That's all before 6 a.m.!

"Come on, come on, let's go, where are they, what's taking so long?" We've all made similar statements from time to time. If we were able to just find a bit more peace in between the crevasses of our "in the future" way of rushing, we'd be giving ourselves a shot at many more moments of enjoyment in life, not to mention mastery of many kinds. Try, my friend, try to add a breath or two in those hurried, seemingly unending minutes of waiting for things to happen.

Pause, wait, stop, hold on, slow down, yield, delay, waiting for answers, being held back by others' speed are all inevitable. These are yet some more good reasons for our breathing conditioning programs.

So Breathe It.

June 4
"FROM" VERSUS "FOR"

"From" versus "for" is what I see as the key to effective prayer and meditation. This concept of *where* we pray "from" makes all the difference. What we want, or pray "for," God already knows. As Jesus taught, we must pray from the abundance, or of the already having. I've seen so often that when people pray, they pray from scarcity, or lack, or not-having. If I learned one thing from Unity (Eric and Olga Butterworth), it was to pray as if it has already been done!

We'd do best to breathe when the voices of doubt, lack of faith, and belief creep in during our prayer time. Breathe in boldness! Not arrogance, but a humble partnering with the Almighty! Again, as Jesus preached, "You too can do these works and much more!" Fish, bread, or anything else, I believe he meant that by coming *from* the Power Within makes all the difference.

Be still and know that I am God. Not ALL of God, but really of and from God.

So Breathe It.

June 5
IT'S AN INSIDE JOB

It's a common belief in recovery that if we are upset it will have something to do with how we are dealing with a given situation; if we take this a step further, our real issues and/or afflictions live within us, and are ultimately acted out in the world. In other words, until we get that "it's an inside job," we'll have difficulty with what it means to be powerless over our shortcomings of procrastination, defiance, and other defects of character. This could have even the best of us taking a deep breath.

When we understand that a problem lives within us, the wisest thing to do is turn to our Higher Power for care and guidance. The negative energy, or the one behind the inside job, doesn't want the boss being brought in. Conscious deep breathing when the underground is rumbling can help our thinking when fear of the unknown comes up.

It was once said, "Take your shoes off when walking upon holy ground." If God is everywhere present, is not all ground holy? It then is a question of respecting the Power and our powerlessness in any and every situation.

So Breathe It.

June 6
THEY ARE ALWAYS WITH US

"They" can mean many different things to many different people. Some days it helps me breathe better when I have thoughts of the dear ones who have gone into the beyond. These are thoughts that they are always with me in ways I'm limited in understanding. Another "they" concerns people who love and care for me and are still here on earth. This too helps me breathe easier knowing they're not that far away.

The most important "they" are the benevolent beings who are helping to heal the planet and humanity. Also my/your Higher Power, and the God of my/your understanding (which may or may not be one and the same), support my overall ease of breath and peace of mind. Knowing and accepting that they are all with us is a leap of faith and belief.

When fear penetrates our minds from within, to "act as if what we want is so," is the best choice in counteracting fearful thinking. Acting "as if" can make all the difference in the face of our challenges.

So Breathe It.

June 7
GYM SIGNS

There are times when I walk into the gym with a preconceived idea of how, what, and where I want to work out. Anyone who exercises in a public arena knows full well that getting what (equipment) we prefer does not always happen. When our expectations are unfulfilled, we need options. This is where I get spiritually connected. Yes, I breathe, as I affirm there is something more appropriate for me to do than I originally thought. Regardless of the venue (a loud, sweaty gym), it is a perfect time for connecting to the Power Within, and turning my will over for guidance is the next right thing to do.

Like a bubble coming up from the depths of water, most of the time the thought of what to do for my workout will show itself within a few relaxed and trusting breaths. If not, I walk around, breathe, and let the guidance come to me in its own time. To me, this is what practicing spirituality (even in a gym) is about.

You walk into a room, God is there with and before you. Breathe. You witness discord, breathe, and affirm Divine order. You notice your own feelings and judgments, breathe in: "this too," breathe out, "shall pass." Then, again inhale: "Thy Will," and exhale, "be done."

So Breathe It.

June 8
TOP BREATHTAKING MOMENTS

Diving, whether it be out of a plane, off a cliff, or tied to a bungee cord, has made the ranks as one of the top 10 breathtaking moments. I am certain that anyone who has done one or more of the above activities doesn't need to be told to take a deep breath. For many of us, however, just watching these activities can propel us into a conscious breathing cycle. Especially if you're watching someone you care for do it.

One of the most traumatizing moments for me was on a high-diving board as a small boy. I was being urged to jump but was terrified. Boy, could I have used someone to guide me in a breathing process then! Being humiliated, I turned and climbed down to the always-loving embrace of my mother, who breathed a sigh of relief that her little boy was OK. Thank you, Mom.

We have tools to go beyond our fears. Yet it is a wise person who knows to listen for what is too much. "No" is a full sentence. It sometimes just comes as a whisper from within. Breathing helps to hear "yes," "no," and "maybe."

So Breathe It.

June 9
WANTING CHANGE

I have yet to meet anyone who was not anxious to change something or another sooner than it was happening. Patience is a life-long skill that we develop, but it is not inborn. Conscious breathing is not the solution, but in my honest opinion, it is the first step toward initiating this all-but-spiritual quality.

When seeking patience, the affirmation I do my best in remembering is: If it is His Will, it will come to pass in His time, not mine. Breathing in, "in His time." Breathing out, "not mine." God knows my urgency in every situation. However, it's not always what's best for all involved. I've found more often than not that the things that eventually do come to pass are better than what I had hoped for. Trust, faith, and patience are born as triplets in the same family.

There are few more valuable life-affirming thoughts than "trust the process." The faith that a mustard seed will become a huge tree, and the promise of the acorn to become a giant oak, are in line with dealing with our perception of time that's needed for things to happen.

So Breathe It.

June 10
WHAT'S MOST IMPORTANT

I've learned through trial and error that my sobriety/sanity is what's most important for me. Without it, nothing matters; ultimately all that is important will be lost if my priority is not soon replaced. My connection with my Higher Power depends directly upon a sane, rational, and sober way of being. When I sacrifice what's most important, my conscious contact with God is first to go. So many times I've had to say my goodbyes due to my indiscretions. This is hard for me to accept and is a very sad growing experience.

Getting back to what's most important usually involves forgiveness on one level or another. As I breathe a few breaths, I do my best to remember that this life of mine is about progress, not perfection. How easy it is to judge ourselves too harshly for being human. God, help me to remember this in my journey back to You. Thank You for the promise of its outcome. Amen.

Forgiveness is the key to my happiness.

So Breathe It.

June 11
BLESS THEM

Blessing someone is not a religious act in itself. Yes, for most of us religion has doctrine and protocol around this act. It is in essence a completely spiritual act. By definition, it is to bestow good of any kind upon a person(s), place, or thing. Good can mean God, protection, healing, making holy, etc.

When we consider giving our blessing, breathing in the thought of what I give out ultimately will come back to me, making blessing a two-way action. Whether we like, dislike, or judge a person harshly, it helps all concerned to share our blessing. It breathes into a person, place, or situation the light of God. It says, "OK, at least one is asking for healing and protection." Depending on the need, forgiveness, benevolence, or surrendering of our will may be called upon.

Anyone can perform a blessing. Priest, rabbi, or holy person—it matters not. Any being with a heart and soul can say yes, I breathe unto you the light of the Universe.

So Breathe It.

June 12
HOLDING OUR BREATH

Have you ever tried to see how long you can hold your breath? No one living can say they've done it for more than a few minutes. However, dozens of my clients have said they find themselves having trouble maintaining regular breaths. Some even say they're not sure how much time goes by without their taking even a single breath! Can you relate to that? Just thinking that thought inspires me to breathe several full conscious breaths.

Here's the fantastic thing about writing and/or reading these words: almost all of us will improve our breathing patterns without even trying. You'll really have to make an effort to not breathe fully and consciously. OK, try again. Reread this last paragraph and don't be aware of your breathing. I assert this is nearly impossible.

It's been said that "there's nothing as powerful as an Idea whose time has come." The Idea here is obvious. The time to breathe is now.

So Breathe It.

These are general survival numbers. Humans can go roughly without breathing for 3 minutes. We also can, give or take, go without water for 3 days; approximately 3 weeks without food. Three seems to be a significant number with respect to our lives. So, why don't we look higher up the scale of self-actualization to life-affirming actions? What if we targeted conditioning our conscious breathing toward every 3 minutes or thereabouts?

We can creatively go further with the number 3 (this number is chosen primarily for the theme being addressed). Our minds are powerful to the point at which if we choose to be reminded to take a breath when we hear or see the number 3, it will become a healthy habit if practiced consistently.

From the most unhealthy to the ultimate in healthy, we are all able to choose our habits. There's so much support to break the destructive ones as well as to encourage the life-giving ones. Ask within, even if you are doubtful. Help can come in the most obvious and sometimes the most mysterious ways.

So Breathe It.

June 14
ONE THING OF SERVICE

So often we go about our days doing things to survive or to get items we want. This is just the way humans are at this point. Some have been taught the value of being of service, or of giving back. It's not that giving is better or more valuable than receiving; it's just healthier if we are balanced. It would be irrational to say that it is better to exhale than it is to inhale. All has been designed to be in a cycle of giving and receiving.

I was taught a gem of wisdom (by W. Erhardt). He would say that when you go into any space, before you leave, attempt to do one thing of service. More often than not it would be known only to yourself. The essence of this I believe was to expand our consciousness to larger, more benevolent ways of existing. Which in turn serves us the most in the end.

To give and to receive are one in truth.

So Breathe It.

June 15
BLOW THE BEAST AWAY

Being as creative as we humans can be, let's use this God-given ability to couple our thoughts with our breathing as we deal with our life challenges.

Let's call my challenge Temptation. As I breathe in, the air vents that were closed in the beast of my temptations room are now opened. It doesn't like anything fresh or clean. My inhale makes it run for cover. When I breathe a full breath out, the door of its room swings open and it is blown out of its place of security. Each time I breathe, the beast loses its foothold of power. I can even see it taking a more relaxed form, and ultimately it changes all of its mean appearances. The final creative vision is the blown-away beast now calm and breathing with me.

One of the pitfalls in being a "mature adult" can be the loss of creative thought to structured, proven, or serious ways of thinking and being. Innocence, not knowing, and spontaneity are childlike qualities that we adults do not have to sacrifice.

So Breathe It.

June 16
REVVING UP

I've had many encounters with people that have not felt nice. Often I may have fanned the flames of unpleasantness by "revving up" my aggression or negativity prior to the interaction. It was as if with each thought I'd become a bit more contracted, tense, righteous, and aggressive. The good news is that there have been times that I've learned to stop, breathe, and give my Higher Power even just a moment to slow the RPM's of my mind down. The velocity of intensity of my mind will of course determine how many conscious breaths are needed in a given situation.

If I'm not aware that I'm building up steam, or revving my mind up for an attack, no amount of breathing will help. I need to be aware that this is what I'm doing. Take a breath. Realize the possible consequences. Take another breath and invite God into my thoughts. Slow down, breathe again, and pray for understanding in my given challenge.

Sometimes I find myself going too fast for my own good. Slowing down may start with taking my foot (or my willfulness) off the accelerator. Putting the brakes on (or forcing myself to change) may be too much too soon. God will show me, if I give Him/Her half a chance.

So Breathe It.

June 17
SOMETHING FROM NOTHING

Authentically creating something truly does seem to come from nothing, and/or apparently from nowhere. That is, from what we can see in the world around us. I like to think our creativity originates from spiritual guides, angels, and God, all having their ways of inspiring us to the awareness of creative thinking. I need to breathe a surrendering breath when I realize that I, or my ego, was not the creator of my inspired vision.

In my prayer time, I breathe the thought to allow my smaller thinking to be gently loosened from its grip on what and how things should be. Like teaching a young child, a persistent approach from a place of compassion can yield the healthiest results in the long run.

God, help me to allow myself to get out of the way and pray. I know You cannot fill the vessel of my mind when it has no room. I now allow what is not bred from love to be released from my heart and soul.

So Breathe It.

June 18
INTERNALIZED AWARENESS

In our world so much of our personal awareness is focused on the outside, or physical, world. Some spiritual masters have called this an imbalance of consciousness being externalized, that is, placing too much energy out here. Of course the physical universe has its supply of amazing, seductive, and baffling things to deal with every day. Just writing these words (let alone reading them), I must pause to breathe. I recommend you do the same.

What more immediate action can you do to internalize your awareness than to have a conscious breath? Yes, closing your eyes will eliminate the visual distractions, but that's not always an appropriate action. The point is to start with your breathing as a portal to focus inside. Your spirit, feelings, God, peace, truth, etc., all can be found within. Seeing from these places, as opposed to just having them, is a lifetime of evolving.

Pray, breathe, lock your doors, meditate, hug someone, have boundaries, trust the process, look both ways before crossing, breathe, share your feelings with a trusted friend, thank God, and yes, breathe again.

So Breathe It.

June 19
DEEP CALM

I believe no matter how crazy my life, the world, and my feelings are, there is a deep calm in the center of my being. It is never anything but peaceful, no matter what's happening outside. To know this with a thought of intense gratitude and a deep breath helps me to live in the moment. This is what I believe has been called a deep eternal peace that lives within all of us and goes beyond our understanding.

When we meditate, pray, and ask our Higher Power for help to return us back to our deep calm, we may not always feel it the way we might like to, but almost always we can take a few steps toward the deep calm by breathing during those actions of going within.

What reminds you of a deep calmness? Is it the first few moments of a sunrise? Being safe inside during a storm? Maybe it's holding a loved one? There are no limits to our creative visualization abilities. Seeing, thinking, and breathing with these things in mind is like an internal navigation system. As the saying goes, "We generally go where we are looking."

So Breathe It.

June 20
BEING OF LOVE

I have been created by God, who is not just loving but is the essence of love and its all-Powerfulness. However the fabric of love looks to you, I (and I believe we) have not only been made from this thread, but it is the very core of who we are. When I see myself or others as being unloving, what a challenge it can be to breathe in the truth of my being when the circumstances speak other than of love. Acting on fear can be such a habit for us. As some of our prophets have said, "You too can do these works as I have, and greater ones." To me there is no greater work than to trust enough to choose love over fear.

In the course of miracles it is said that all things come from either love or fear. This can be tough to understand when we try to apply this to all our circumstances. However, it is absolutely accurate. One example is when I have constrictive breathing and/or am being tense, fear of opting for a compassionate perception of things may look like getting angry, rather than understanding.

If we are to be able to move a mountain by our faith, the ground upon which we move it to and from will certainly be grounded on love. It is safe and natural for me to love and be loved.

So Breathe It.

June 21
SCULPTING SOULS

What if our souls come to this world to be shaped or sculpted into greater beings to become more loving and brighter beacons of light? Our tools of affirmations, conscious breathing, and living in the moment can be seen as chisels. These mechanisms over a lifetime give more breath to our souls in everyday experiences. In turn, this may carve us into more magnificent God-centered beings.

It helps me breathe easier imagining that each and every earthly experience contributes to my becoming more able to express my divine nature. Every time I have a conscious breath, I relax my body so the flow of healing life can gain more access to each cell. On a deeper level, just the consciousness to slow down, let go, and be here now has a soul-sculpting quality that has its greatest impact over a full lifetime.

I am not the ultimate artist, musician, or designer. Allowing my mind, body, and spirit to be shaped by the Divine is very much based on my willingness. Letting God's image come forth is just another way of saying Thy Will Be Done!

So Breathe It.

June 22
MY INTERNAL DASHBOARD

As with a car, the internal dashboard gives us vital information for safe, efficient driving. Drivers generally use a quick look at the dashboard for only three or four things that are essential during movement. There's no question of the value of conscious breaths while driving. However, the idea of what would be on my internal dashboard recently came to mind. What are the three or four important bits of information that would help me have a safer, healthier, and happier experience of life?

Definitely one would be the love/fear meter. Another could be the breathing/not breathing gauge. My WAIT acronym has two readings: Where Am I Tense? And, What Am I Thinking? Last but not least would be the "my will/Thy Will" barometer. All of these readouts have a common response mechanism. First and foremost the reaction would be to breathe and then make healthy adjustments.

Signs and messages are constantly given to all of us. How, when, and where to see them can always be improved upon. As with driving a car, the awareness of our breathing can help to see and respond to the communications from within.

So Breathe It.

June 23
TAKING THE GARBAGE OUT

In the 12 Step and the 12 Principle programs, the tenth step/principle deals with continuing to take personal inventories and making healthy safe adjustments when needed. Taking away the dirty stigma of garbage, we can then see it as simply discarding used and unnecessary items. By doing this, we can more readily equate this process of taking out the garbage to our thoughts, feelings, and actions that need to be recycled or disposed of.

Sometimes just taking a deep breath and admitting that I'm feeling hurt over something is all that's needed to take the hurt feeling and recycle it into an opportunity. If I need to still be with an item, it is not ready to be taken out to the trash bin. Breathing in and around thoughts and feelings can help us to see what they're showing us. The sooner this happens, the sooner we can move forward.

This too shall pass.

So Breathe It.

June 24
PRAY UNCEASINGLY

It's been said that our thoughts are prayers. If that's the case, choosing our thoughts becomes a whole different ballgame. For the religiously inclined, that means God hears all our thoughts and in turn, responds to them. For the ones who lean toward metaphysics, they tend to be a bit less judgmental, but still all thoughts are seen as energy that is responded to by returning back to us what we give out. In either school of thought, breathing before, during, and after our praying/thinking can give us that needed moment or two of reflection.

If there were one thought/prayer I default to during my days, it would have to be, *Thy Will Be Done,* or as I personally prefer to say it, *may our Wills be one.* Right up there with the non-denominational /.non-judgmental thought, of course would be *BREATHE.*

For one to say pray unceasingly in essence is saying God/the Universe hears and responds to all thoughts and actions. This could be considered good or bad news, but knowing everything counts can give us a sense of power that is unlimited in its capacity.

So Breathe It.

June 25
LET IT BE

The late John Lennon is well known for the phrase "Let it be". He was definitely speaking words of wisdom when he wrote them. Thousands, maybe tens of thousands of times I would have been wise to just let things be. To have breathed in the words *let it* and breathed out *be* . . . In our hours of darkness, we allow the Mother of Mercy to come to us when we let things be just the way they are.

"It" can mean just about anything to anyone. To let it be means to not try to shape, manipulate, or change anything in any way. Being a culture of doers, we're trained to make things happen. See it, believe it, and do it. Rediscovering the realm of just being can start right now for you. Breathe, and just let everything just be the way it is, even for a few moments.

Whether we agree or like it, everything is just being the way it is. Our consciousness and perception would benefit if we just let things be the way they are. Change can and will happen later.

So Breathe It.

June 26
THE JOURNEY HOME

If we see home as being where the heart is, then our passion, love, and spirit all can make wherever we are "home." It can be almost impossible to bring these qualities into every day, let alone into every moment. For our purposes, let's call our pathway back to a passionate, loving, and spiritual way of living the journey home. When I notice I'm feeling like a stranger, no matter where I am, I breathe and remember I can experience right here and now as home.

We can also look at our entire lives as a journey home, the challenge of returning back to where we came from. There's a theory that in reality we never leave our true God-given home. That our soul or spirit resides within the center of our beings throughout life. The very thought brings a comforting full breath to me. No matter the problems or destruction in our lives, our true home is intact and awaiting our arrival in consciousness.

Any sort of enlightenment/transformation in my life has always been accompanied by a more profound sense of "being at home" exactly where and how I'm being. I suppose when I move into the beyond, it will be one of the most exquisite experiences of returning back to where I had never left.

So Breathe It.

June 27
RELEASING THE EGO

I've heard the ego's primary job is to get us across the street alive. That means its function is our survival. Other than that, we can see a trillion times over how much trouble our ego can cause if we let it become the decision maker. In other words, it is the perfect servant, but the worst master. For me, I need to breathe deep when I realize just how often my ego is trying its best to run the show. I may not be sure if I've allowed it to get its hands on the steering wheel, but I'm always certain it's trying to wheedle its way in.

The story of the fallen angel is of how the devil was once an angel, but it didn't want to serve God so it fell from grace to cause havoc. The story is a perfect metaphor for us and our egos. The Divine challenge is to not only make friends with our enemy but to learn to harness its energy for life-affirming actions in life. In the light of this apparently unending process, I breathe and recommend you do the same.

In my release is everyone's peace.

So Breathe It.

June 28
EVERY GLANCE COUNTS

As every penny we spend has an impact on our finances, every thought has an effect in our life and affairs. One topic that's infrequently addressed is what we look, glance, or stare at. When I drive past an accident and look at the trauma, it has an effect on me. When I walk down the street only to glance (or stare) at a woman's body, which is called objectification, it also has its cost on my peace. It may sound petty, but every glance, stare, and moment of intrigue has its taxation on the moments we choose to indulge. Each of us has our own personal integrity to manage. Some are more affected by what they drink in with their eyes, yet others can be devastated by what they drink into their bodies.

When I get into debating whether I'm living with a sense of integrity, I pause to breathe and know that if the committee in my mind has to debate about it, more often than not it's time to be honest, breathe, and move on.

So Breathe It.

June 29
GIVE PEACE A CHANCE

After John Lennon was sadly taken from our community, I vividly remember chanting in New York's Central Park. With tears in our eyes, we repeatedly sang out: "All we are saying, is give peace a chance." Now almost 35 years later, as I walk past the Dakota (the last building he lived in) and into the part of the park called Strawberry Field (where John's memorial spot is), I breathe a heavy breath. What an icon of peace he was. The ones who grew up with and around him still miss him a lot.

A whimpering breath is all I have when I think of the cruelty of violence, war, and hurting each other. God, I know You have the big plan in Divine order, but sometimes I need to breathe through the hatred of how it is unfolding. Then another choked-up breath through the tears. And then finally a breath of acceptance of the way our world is now.

The peace that lives deep within all of us, if given a chance, will take root individually, communally, and globally. I have faith and trust that it is happening in this very moment. I refuse to believe differently!

So Breathe It.

June 30
URBAN ETHICS: ON THE BUS

Some days I have to laugh at just how many things present themselves to be dealt with on the bus. I breathe as I try my best to step around the person wearing the backpack who's taking up most of the aisle. But yet another breath is needed sitting down next to the person who has the sense of entitlement to take up part of my seat. I tell myself, "OK, Scott, breathe again, it's just someone speaking a bit too loudly on their phone for your comfort. The phone is nothing compared to the person drinking hot coffee next to me on this unsteady ride. Breathe and trust the process, Scott."

The previous paragraph may sound a bit negative, but if you've ever ridden on a busy NYC bus, the portrayed monologue in my head was quite positive. OK, here's the Urban Ethic: when on a public bus please remember this is not your living room; being considerate of others' riding experience contributes to the overall peace and fluidity of the city. Thank you for your consideration. Breathe, Scott.

As the biblical saying goes, "Do unto others as you would have them do unto you." Or one of the philosophies that gives me a breath of peace is: "What goes around comes around." Amen.

So Breathe It.

July 1
BLESS THE FOOD

I have had to let go of the ritual of praying and blessing food before a meal. I know that most religions follow the tradition of saying grace, but I have never felt right reciting any kind of prayer that didn't come from my heart in any given moment. That being said, I close my eyes and breathe in order to let go of being too outside or physically focused. I affirm God's love that originally created and got the food to me. I breathe again as I visualize any and all less than healthy things in the food being cleansed with the healing light of the Universe. Then maybe a thought of gratitude and loving silence for those who may be hungry as I eat.

Thank You, God. For your original ideas of nourishment and for the billions of years needed to make a planet to produce and support the growth of food, I breathe a thought of extreme gratitude. In the beginning You may have said, "lLet there be light," and in turn this was needed to grow the food with which I now can fill my belly. Thank You. Amen.

So Breathe It.

July 2
A MOMENT OF SILENCE

When we're asked to spend a moment of silence for a person or persons, it's a totally different experience for each person. Of course the first thing I do in order to do nothing is to breathe. After that I have a better chance to be in silence not so much as a sign of respect but as a means of surrounding them in the light that I wish to send them. I've heard that when we pray or meditate with good intentions toward someone who is no longer with us, they get the love and light on the level at which they are now able to receive it. It never goes undelivered—or unreceived.

The next time you have the opportunity to spend a moment of silence remembering someone you cared for, maybe it will give both you and that person a moment of light, love, and healing. Has it not been said that we can't give what we do not have already?

I am not only created from God's light and love, but I am a beacon for all who need to see the shore in all its changing conditions. I do my best to maintain my lighthouse so I can give out illumination for all to live, grow, and prosper from. In that moment of silence, the light has no bounds.

So Breathe It.

July 3
GOD KNOWS

Along with "God help me," or "us," or "them," "God knows" is probably one of the most uttered phrases throughout humanity. Whether we believe in God or not, most of us tend to refer to Him/Her in times of great need. I breathe easier believing that God does indeed know everything I don't have access to at any given moment. Furthermore, my gut says there's no knowledge I'm restricted to, but I am given knowledge based on my conditioning to receive and process it. In my pursuit to know things, it might be better to say (rather than "God knows") in my next few quiet breaths, if it's best for all concerned, "I'm willing to know."

God is omnipresent, omniscient, and omnipotent; therefore, as one of my favorite affirmations says, "There is no spot where God is not." And, "Never fear, God is here." And, on a lighter note, "God is alive, He just doesn't want to get involved."

So Breathe It.

July 4
YES, NO, MAYBE

When somebody asks me a complicated question that could only have a complex answer, I've been known to sincerely say (to the irritation of some people), "yes, no, maybe." I've not told many what I recently understood about myself, but it will explain in part why I answer so all-inclusively. This is it: I used to think I was quite smart; now, I know better. I personally need to breathe after writing that disclosure to you. My ego didn't like that admission one bit.

On a more esoteric and spiritual note, for any fact we question, depending on our perspective and perception, "yes, no, maybe" fits the bill. Does the Universe go on forever? Yes, no . . . Am I a loving person? Yes, no, maybe. The point is more than my giving an answer that I think I know; my response enables the questioner to reevaluate what and why they are asking me. So many times I've given an answer only to be left holding my breath.

I know nothing, and I trust myself completely. That covers it all as well.

So Breathe It.

July 5
JUST THE WAY I AM

We can put many words in front of "just the way I am," and it would be equally challenging to believe the phrase, whatever it is. "I love myself just the way I am." Before I finish the first four or five words, I can hear the committee in my head saying: "Yes, but what about . . . and you really don't if . . ." OK, let me try an easier thing: "I accept myself just . . ." "No you don't. What about when you did . . . and said . . ." Boy, there's so little I can honestly attach to that phrase and really mean it, let alone not have to justify it! You know what I'm doing now, yes, taking a deep breath as I affirm: "I'm doing the best I can to accept my flaws just the way they are."

There are so many sayings that are helpful to remind us not to be too hard on ourselves. Why not read each one of the following statements and challenge yourself to breathe a breath in-between each one.

Progress, not perfection.
Easy does it.
I'm a work in progress.
I'm God's living enterprise, and God doesn't fail.
God loves and accepts me no matter what.

So Breathe It.

July 6
THE BIG MEETING

All of us have big meetings with people whom we may want or need to impress. Each will vary in importance, yet if it's one whose outcome is significant to us, our breathing habits will have a big effect on our stress levels. Two actions we know can positively impact heart rate and blood pressure are thinking and breathing. A primary reason for having and using an effective breathing conditioning program is to enable you to deal with big meetings that may come up. You need to think clearly before and during these meetings. Sufficient oxygen supply to your brain and body will stack the deck in your favor.

It is also apparent to most people when we are tense: when you limit your breathing, your voice sounds different; your muscles are programmed to constrict due to a survival mechanism as well. As you can see, meditation, prayer, exercise, eating, and breathing habits are very much a part of the world of business, of money, and of survival.

Gratitude is the universal law of supply (this was demonstrated by Jesus with fish, wine, and bread a long time ago). Thank You, God, for this meeting. I am grateful for Your guidance before, during, and after this important experience. Amen.

So Breathe It.

July 7
BEING IN THE ZONE

Athletes, artists, musicians, and just about anyone who is doing a task with maximum focus can speak of what it's like to "be in the zone." Science describes it as having the Alpha and Beta waves balanced within our brains. Getting to and remaining in this zone seems to be a productive practice, as well as a safe and healthy place to be in.

There are several things that certainly help to bring us to the zone, as well as many that definitely would work against staying in it. Because this is quite a meditative experience, relaxed breathing would be a given; a relaxed focus with few or no permitted distractions would also be included. Being judgmental, evaluating our feelings, preoccupation with the past or the future, and, most assuredly, restricted/minimal breathing would work against our zone-worthiness.

In Zen philosophy it is expressed as "Just do the task at hand, with nothing added." Along these lines, it may help to become aware of the truth that your breathing is just breathing; your body in essence is just being still while performing its functions, and your mind is simply just thinking what it is thinking. Being in the zone boils down to allowing or letting things be just the way they are.

So Breathe It.

July 8
ON BORROWED TIME

The fact that most of the men in my family died of heart disease at about the age I am now puts me in a high risk category. Yes, I'm seen as having a much healthier lifestyle, but being in the world of recovery in addition to my life experiences, I often see myself as living on borrowed time. As I breathe into this perception, I see it as having positive and negative effects in me. At times I feel the stress of worry about the future, but, on the other hand, this knowledge helps me to live in the moment, breathe, and be grateful for what I have and do not have.

Seeing myself as living on borrowed time is helping me not only to understand the importance of living the best I can each day, but, very tangibly, to finish the Daily Breath book, just in case. Try taking a relaxing breath now and think if there is something you'd like to start or finish, just in case.

Dear God, I know You've granted me the serenity to accept the things I cannot change. I thank You for my strength to change the things I'm meant to change; access to Your infinite wisdom to make healthy choices. Amen.

So Breathe It.

July 9
NO FREE LUNCH

"No free lunch" is a philosophy of one of the original recovery organizations. At first it may seem quite a negative statement. When you understand it from a health and fitness perspective, it can be helpful when navigating through the unending supply of products and services. As we look honestly at what the industry so often promises, let's breathe deeply. If something is offered that entails a miraculous pill, a promise of results in a few minutes a day, or cutting of any corners toward your health and fitness, take another breath and understand there is a very strong probability that something is amiss.

We can also translate this aphorism into spiritual or metaphysical understanding as well. The energy that we send out in our lives/Universe is the payment or investment that most definitely will be returned to us at some point or another. Pleading with God or hoping for results without the energy/work/payment backing your wish can be equated to expecting a free lunch.

To give and to receive are one in truth; or, as you sow, so shall you reap.

So Breathe It.

July 10
FROM THE HIGHEST POINT OF VIEW

To see life from the highest point of view is one of the most valuable metaphysical teachings I've learned to this point in my life. In one word, it's about choice. We are always free to choose the perspective or place from which we process or view our lives. Can it be put more simply than what many of us have heard—to see the glass half empty, or half full. Let's take a few moments to breathe; see where each of us can climb up the ladder of our perception to view from a healthier, loftier, and more positive place what is happening to and around us.

God, I am now willing to let go and see my life as You will for me. I know I can always have the next higher thought toward seeing all as the unfolding of the ultimate good for all, even if it doesn't look or feel that way presently. When I breathe, it's much easier to let go of my smaller thinking. Thank You for this truth. Amen.

So Breathe It.

July 11
BRAND NEW

Your next breath is brand new, never experienced in the way you're having it right now. But, really, it has already happened, so now it's your next breath that indeed is brand new once again. Here's a healthy game or challenge for yourself. For the next several breaths, be with this thought: what is it about my current breath that I experience as brand new?

I recently bought a new car. The interior smell of fresh leather, the shiny black paint, and the tightness of all the working parts during a drive all contributed to the joyful newness. Then came the first scratch on the trunk. Thanks to my best friend, who reminded me of The Daily Breath, I breathed into my upset and was able to remember what was more important in life. Anything I would allow to take me away from my conscious connection with God needs to be put in perspective. Thanks, Laura, for helping me to remember that.

In God all is brand new in His eternal moment of life. He has freely given angels and guides to all of His children to assist in learning to enjoy each new moment. Thank You, God, for these gifts of love.

So Breathe It.

July 12
JUST FOR TODAY

It can be extremely overwhelming to think too far into the future. If there's one thing that adds to limiting my breathing it's worrying or putting too much thinking time toward tomorrow or yesterday. Spirituality, recovery, business, or relationships, all have pretty much the same importance when we talk about living just for today. Fear of the future or regrets from the past are equally depleting to us. It is commonly said that your worries about tomorrow almost always are never justified; the past is over, it cannot hurt you unless you let it.

Let's slowly inhale, whispering "just," and, even slower, breathing out the words "for today." Try it a few times; you might be surprised at what that statement can do with regard to the joy of being alive today. Give us this day our daily bread (or Daily Breath), not tomorrow, but today. Tomorrow will take care of itself. In truth, we can only be in this moment. It is always the eternal now. Moreover, once we think about the moment it's over.

God, help me to help myself live in recovery from whatever ails me, just for today. Please lift my obsession about tomorrow, for it most certainly will take care of itself. Amen.

So Breathe It.

July 13
HEALING A BROKEN HEART

If there's a range of emotions that can make breathing a challenge, it's grief, loss, and deep sadness. Being crippled as a young boy, losing my mother to cancer when I was 11 years old, and having my share of relationship breakups, I'm no stranger to what it's like to have to force air into my lungs due to the heaviness of a broken heart. If you're in that place now, the beacon of love and concern that's here with The Daily Breath is sent to you many times over.

Saying or hearing "this too shall pass," as true as it may be, can be like water running off a duck's back during a storm. Be with the hurt, breathe, you're never alone, feel your feelings—these are just some of the words and phrases that can prove helpful during these most challenging experiences. Sometimes I have to smile when I hear "one day at a time," because it's more real to be with one breath, or even one moment at a time.

In my life there has not yet been true growth without hurt, pain, and discomfort. In the deepest experiences of those, all we can manage is one breath, and then to reach for one more, and so on.

So Breathe It.

July 14
HIGH HOLY DAYS

Most religions have their high holy days. I believe that it is our choice to see each day as a high holy day, a day given to us as a gift from the highest and holiest of all, our Creator. Holidays are made by humans, who also have the ability to hold each day of his or her life as a holy day. Breathing into this opportunity, a shift in our perception is all that's needed. No need to get down on our knees to thank the Lord (unless that feels right for you), but to breathe in the possibility that there is another way of looking at life every day. Seeing an all-ness or wholeness, that is the essence of a holiday, today!

The human race has many days made for special devotion and reverence to God, and manmade honoring rituals called holy days (holidays). As individuals we are able to not only create any day to honor whatever we choose but can devote any and all moments toward the salutation of God on down. In order to salute or give reverence, we must first get it, or them, into our consciousness. So in our breathing, I pose to all of us to be as God-centered as possible so we can make each moment/day a holy-day.

Namaste, the divinity in me salutes the divinity in you.

So Breathe It.

July 15
SINCERELY YOURS

The definition of being sincere is to be free of deceit, to be genuine, real, pure, and unadulterated. For many of us, this can instigate a sincere deep breath when analyzing situations in our past when we thought we were truly being sincere. With regard to signing a letter "Sincerely yours," I've concluded hundreds in this fashion. In retrospect, I can count on one hand the number of times there was complete integrity in those words. My ego is having a tantrum by admitting that. Before I write on, I'm taking a few humbling breaths.

As far as God, me, my Higher Power, angels, and guides go, there is not a hint of doubt when I say "sincerely yours." This thought brings on a breath of comfort and compassion. Knowing in my heart of hearts that they see all can be refreshingly disarming. Considering that we are bred from and are made in a like image of our Creator, it follows suit that underneath all the distractions we too know the sincerity of each other. I'm not sure what type of breath it is, but I find myself breathing deep from those words as well.

In Truth, we are all One. In "Truth," secrets have nowhere to hide. God, grant me the sincerity to live my life with complete integrity. Sincerely Yours, Your son. Amen.

So Breathe It.

July 16
LTD

LTD are the initials of a woman friend in my life. Without her love, professionalism, and creative skills, in all probability this book would have never made it out of my head for publication. She's in all of my prayers of gratitude toward trusting God to provide love and support. She has reminded me to breathe almost as many times as you may read it on these pages. If you are getting value from The Daily Breath, having a breath of thankfulness for what LTD has provided for you through me would be supportive to all of us.

Is there a person in your life, or a person who has been in your life, for whom you could easily have a few breaths and thoughts of gratitude when thinking about them? The person whose compassionate support has enabled you to be a better person is the one we're breathing better because of. It's my belief most people have had an angel in their lives like LTD is and has been for me. If you haven't yet, my prayers of hope and faith that your angel is coming to you is my gift to you right now!

Just as we would prepare our home for a guest, so it is wise to do the same in consciousness for our oncoming angels, protectors, and guides.

So Breathe It.

July 17
PURE ENERGY

When I recently heard the term "pure energy," I then wondered what it really meant. Being who I am, I defaulted to thinking in terms of the unseen forms rather than the physical types of energy. To make a long definition short, this is what I came up with: It's the Universal Life Force with nothing added. So when I breathe during a relaxing meditation, I am literally letting go of the tension or blockages that may inhibit the flow of Universal Life to cells, organs, and all functions.

Is there anything more pure than God's energy, which makes cells work, protons and neutrons circle each other, and the planets stay in orbit? This would include the energy and programming required for our continuous breathing, whether we're conscious of it or not. While we're at it, let's throw into the mix the Life Energy that's needed for our hearts to beat every moment of our lives. Talking about God's pure Life Energy helps us to realize just how much of it there is in every spot. As goes one of my favorite affirmations: "There is no spot where God is not."

No ifs, ands, or buts, God is everywhere! Amen!

So Breathe It.

July 18
GOD'S LIVING ENTERPRISE

There are times when we all feel like failures, less than expected, or just not enough for someone or something. It's taken me most of my life to accept the fact that wading through these feelings is what growing is all about. There have been countless times when I was not pleased with myself or my actions only to be breathing deep in a moment of surrender. A letting go of my unfulfilled expectations was needed before I could move forward and open to genuine forgiveness to all involved.

Everybody needs different amounts of time for hurting and healing. Whether it be mental, emotional, or physical, we are all designed to move toward healing. God made us this way. I need to remember this so often. Fighting the process will only hamper my return to peace and wholeness. I pray that we all can let go and let God do His work in and through us now, and forever more. Amen.

We are all God's living enterprises, and God does not fail.

So Breathe It.

July 19
NOT HAPPENING THAT WAY

I was sitting in a meeting recently, and a person shared that he had put a message on his refrigerator that said: "It's not going to happen that way!" The group giggled, and the person went on to say he had put another message on his bathroom mirror that said: "It's not going to happen that way either!" Then the group began laughing quite loudly. I believe the point was that our minds are constantly trying to figure out how things are going to happen in life; and the funny thing was how the two messages hit home twice that the person's mind was going to be reminded not to expect things.

I often must go back to my breathing as a calming source when my expectations are unfulfilled. Usually it's an intense feeling that breathing helps to loosen my grip on. I'm not trying to deny my feelings but rather to get them in a healthy perspective. Then and only then can I have a chance at staying in the present moment.

As one of my favorite buttons states: Create Miracles, Breathe!

So Breathe It.

July 20
INFLAMED

Injuries, irritations, and infections are what we associate with being inflamed or with inflammation. Always a bodily sign to be heeded. However, my definition of In-flamed is about being focused inward. It's a commonly used meditation technique to help us calm our minds by looking at the flame of a candle, or envisioning one with closed eyes.

The fact that the flame needs oxygen to burn can be a gentle reminder for us to consciously breathe in the oxygen we need. Also, the flame can remind us of God's energy that makes a flame possible, not to mention the ultimate flame (the sun) as being the source of energy that makes our life on earth possible. Let's allow the flame to symbolize the constant flow of life that God has freely given us all.

Thank You, God, for Your warmth that takes on so many forms in our lives. We've all read that You said "Let there be light" and that it was good. We're realizing just how good it is! Amen.

So Breathe It.

July 21
BENCHMARK DAY

We all have days that get that special notch on the workbench of our lives. There's nothing quite like the empowered kind of deep breath that comes at the end of a Benchmark Day. It's a day that we'll never forget. God doesn't either. For that matter, I believe He/She knew it was coming all along! These are the days that help keep us going when storms in our lives cloud over the ever-present light of God. Thank Him/Her for the reminders that come in a multitude of forms.

Here's a rhetorical question for us: What would it take to make this a benchmark life? My assertion is that it would be more in the form of where we come from, rather than what we were to accomplish. Let's wake up in the morning, regardless of what we're feeling, and tell ourselves that this is the day I'm not going to hold back. Live this day as if there were no tomorrow.

THIS IS IT! We don't get a dress rehearsal for this life. This really is it! Let us be so empowered in our thought and breath that remembering that this really is It becomes the tool with which we create this life to the best of our ability.

So Breathe It.

July 22
GPS

Global Positioning Satellites (GPS) are a familiar term to our society. They help us find our way in cars, when hiking, and in many other situations. I've transformed the term to fit my spiritual needs. I see GPS as God's Positioning Spirit. When I breathe, check my internal dashboard, and have a place to start from, God's spirit can guide me no matter where I'm going or what I wish to accomplish. My intentions are not important when using the global satellite. The requirements for use are tuning in and responding to its guidance.

Is it not quite the same as receiving guidance from our Source of Life from within? We each have our own way of tuning in, or shutting out the noise that may block our guidance. Breathing, closing our eyes, relaxing the body, visualizing, prayer, and most important, waiting for the revealing of Thy Will are necessary. As with most skills, these preparatory steps improve with practice over our lifetime.

The quality of our letting go and letting God show us the way improves throughout our lives with practice.
Be still and know that you are being guided always, in all ways.

So Breathe It.

July 23
ATTITUDE OF GRATITUDE

The title of this Daily Breath has a nice rhyme to it, but moreover it has deep value. In short, our attitude is the mental disposition we bring into a given situation. A thankful attitude or disposition brings forth an energy of appreciation, joy, and acknowledgment. How life-affirming it would be to breathe gratitude into all our experiences. Even the painful and upsetting ones always have room for a thankful thought that things could be worse. When we have an attitude of gratitude we remain open to more prosperity on every level. Prospering is not exclusive to money by any means. When we are given things from God on down we prosper.

So often we hear of keeping a gratitude list. What a powerful tool! Just the act of thinking and writing what we are grateful for gets us into that receptive energy of receiving more. Here's another way of physically getting into the energy of gratitude: Breathe the air out of your lungs and wait 10 seconds before inhaling. This is an immediate jump start experience of thankfulness. The number one physical need we all are most grateful for is the air we breathe.

Gratitude is the law of supply! Thank You, God, for all that I have, and all that I don't have. Amen.

So Breathe It.

July 24
HITTING THE WALL

Marathon runners are familiar with "hitting the wall" at about the 20-mile point. It's the place where the challenge is at its greatest intensity. The feeling that he just can't go on any further seems to grip the runner with all its oppressive force. My belief is that there's not an adult person alive who has not had the experience of feeling they could not make it, or go on in life anymore.

We can now breathe in the truth about our capabilities of endurance. Seeing as you and I are still here, it was the Will of God (and still is) to carry us through even the toughest of times. We were made to not only endure but to prosper and enjoy! Let's breathe a joyous breath about that fact! If you're in the midst of a trying time, know that better times are coming.

To know the truth that sets us free is but part of that prophetic teaching. To believe in it, trust it, breathe it, live by it, and share it, is what it means to completely know the truth that sets us free.

So Breathe It.

July 25
DIAMOND IN THE ROUGH

I was recently watching a science and nature show that was showing how a diamond is created. It struck me how similar my process of growth is to that of a diamond. The amount of incredible pressure that is put on relatively valueless elements for a prolonged duration of time eventually makes a diamond a diamond. From basic carbon elements it becomes a spectacular reflector of light and color.

From the uncomfortable, and sometimes extreme, pressure of life on life's terms, our spirits become greater beacons to reflect or channel God's life, light, and love into the world. Is this not one of the most spectacular abilities or functions we can demonstrate in this world that needs this healing life? Knowing that the ones who help me through my challenges have endured similar pressures reminds me to breathe a breath of faith and hope.

It was said that his yoke was easy and his burden was light. Before he earned that way of being, I'm sure he learned to deal with the pressures of life, which were anything but light and easy.

So Breathe It.

July 26
YOU'RE THE GIFT

My girlfriend and I were going to visit her aunt, who was not feeling well. We wanted to bring a gift to help lift her spirits, but we weren't sure what she'd like. Out of nowhere I said, "Honey, you're the gift!" It's a funny thing, but as soon as we both got clear on what was the real gift, what we wanted to buy came to us quickly. Looking back at that experience has validated the importance of getting and remaining clear on what's most valuable in life.

Making the effort, showing up, and our presence more often than not will be what's most valued by the ones we care for. When I go to visit my friends and family, I breathe in the truth that I'm what they treasure most. The material gifts are important, yet they're mere representations of the love that is intended to move them. In all of my memories of gatherings, I don't recall most of the gifts given. It was the loved ones who were there, I remember most.

The list of gifts in our lives is a very long one. They all can be seen as having their origin in God. As He breathed life into you, as you, so He continues to bestow His treasures upon you.

So Breathe It.

July 27
BECOMING QUIET

Once we accept that our minds will never stop thinking, becoming quiet takes on a new meaning. For instance, if we are aware of our breathing, the volume of our thoughts begins to somehow decrease. Yet if we interact or dialogue with our thoughts, it's like being in a room where two or more people are talking at once. The choice to not react, evaluate, or judge what our minds are thinking is the prerequisite to becoming quiet and peaceful amid the noise.

Stepping back and detaching from what's happening in and around us doesn't mean that we don't care or have an opinion. It just means that we're giving ourselves breathing space for peace and quiet to be the focus of our attention. It is the conscious intention to breathe and acknowledge that there's peace within our being that goes far beyond our understanding.

Sitting by a flowing river can be relaxing. Its appearance may be loud and active, yet somehow it elicits a peaceful feeling in us. We don't have to understand how the river works, but if we're not struggling within it, we can quietly flow with it.

So Breathe It.

July 28
EVERYTHING BUT THE KITCHEN SINK

There are times when I exercise and I'm very tired or just not into it. I have a technique for those times that often helps to jump start my energy and motivation. I allow myself to do any exercise that I feel like in the moment. Usually it's very light weights and easy motions that allow me to enjoy movement without exerting too much effort. I kid you not, almost always there's a movement that gets me going on all levels. Sometimes it takes a while, but permitting myself to not be forced into a routine often does the trick.

On a spiritual/emotional/mental level, I sometimes look for a thought or affirmation to help me through a trying time. However, there are times when it feels like I've tried everything but the kitchen sink to no avail. That's when I apply the exercise technique to my thoughts, prayers, and affirmations. I allow myself to use anything that comes into my mind as a vehicle toward getting centered and grounded. It may sound something like this:

Breathe, let go of that thought, and just take another breath. God, help me to help myself. This feeling of hurt and pain will pass soon. What I resist shall persist. I'm willing to release my anger now. Breathe, Scott, feeling like I am not doing this right is not bad. The truth of my being is that I am of God, and the more I breathe that truth into my awareness, the more I will live that truth. Amen.

So Breathe It.

July 29
CHOOSE LIFE

The phrase "choose life" can mean something different to each person interpreting it. When The Daily Breath reminds us to breathe, in essence it is supporting us to choose life. When we restrict or limit our respiration/breathing, to a certain extent we're cutting the flow of life to our cells. When we take a conscious breath and it enables us to think in a sane, sober, and safe way, this too is choosing life on a less direct, yet equally profound level.

When we commune with God/the Life Force Within during meditation or prayer, is this not the highest way to choose life? If we adhere to the belief that gratitude is the law of supply, when we thank our Creator for the very life that has been given to us, are we not affirming, choosing, and increasing the supply of life? In short, by getting into the flow of the Universal Life Force through our thoughts and actions, we are indeed choosing life.

It has been said in our holy books that by giving thanks for what we have, we can increase our supply to have enough to go around for all in need. Thank You, God, for my life. I now choose to be a channel of Your healing life energy. Amen.

So Breathe It.

July 30
MONEY

I think most of us would agree that the subject of money can test even the most spiritually inclined person in his or her attachments to the material world. If we remember the supreme affirmation on the one-dollar bill (In God We Trust), we most certainly would breathe easier in most money matters. When I give or pay money out, I do my best to breathe into this affirmation: I release this money knowing much more is coming back to me. If I resist this truth, I try my best to recall that money has always come to me, over and over again.

In my spiritual/metaphysical trainings I've been taught that humans are constantly gathering evidence. We have a position or belief and then proceed to look for the justifications in order to be validated. We're all going to continue gathering one way or the other. It may take a bit of honesty and conscious breathing to realize just how free we are to choose our beliefs and, moreover, to change them if they stop serving us. What are your beliefs surrounding money? Are they ones that you want to keep or change?

Do I really trust in God? My breathing will almost always indicate if I'm in a trusting place or not.
Prosperity consciousness can start with a penny, a thought, or a charitable action.
To give and to receive are one in truth.

So Breathe It.

July 31
BREATH-TAKING

I'm sure all movie-watching adults have found themselves holding their breath on more than one occasion. Without getting into judging and evaluating the mental and emotional effects of viewing shows that are geared toward creating fear, stress, and tension, the next time you find yourself holding your breath during what you're watching, it is my prayer that you take a few breaths based on your breathing conditioning from these Daily Breath readings.

My appetite for tense, scary, and/or violent movies has decreased over the years. However, I'm part of the human community and still am entertained by Hollywood filmmaking. I believe a big difference between me and most people being entertained is that I probably take it too seriously for the fantasy/fun it's meant to be. I use the visceral effects being triggered as a sign to not get caught up in the illusive part of life. The blood, the explosions, and the mean intentions bring me back to my breathing as a tool of peace and health.

In my release, I find the peace that has never left, the peace that cannot be marred or diminished in any way by the physical universe. Thank God for this truth that lives within all of us. Amen.

So Breathe It.

August 1
DAILY BREATH FOR SCOTT

Scott [substitute your own name], breathe. Can we take another breath in such a way that it transports our awareness to a loftier, more spirit-based place? If not, it's OK to ask our Higher Power to help us. God, honestly, I know it's best to let go now, but what I'm experiencing has got me out of synch with You. It concerns me to say Thy Will Be Done, because I don't feel it's completely honest. I speak a good game, but I'm doubting my ability to turn even the simplest things over to You.

This is what I believe God wants to say to us:

Breathe, Scott [substitute your own name]. You're here to heal, grow, and serve. There's no timetable for this to occur. It has been and may continue to be a messy path, but that's expected. Each conscious breath you take allows you a few more precious moments of my life given to you. If your breathing brings you more than that, hallelujah! No need to rush back home. I've always been here and will always be here for you, when and only when you're ready to return. For this truth we breathe together and say, Amen.

So Breathe It.

August 2
LOOKING GOOD

There is a saying that "when you think you're looking good, you're really not, and when you think you're looking bad, you're really not." With an awareness of the part our ego often plays in our lives, this philosophy makes a lot of sense. There are times when I think "I'm all that," and that's when I need to take a breath and come back to the reality of my life, which is healing, recovery, and service. When I get back in touch with my life's purpose, I can leave being "all that" to Hollywood stars, professional athletes, and my cats.

Oh, for the record there's only one who holds the position of being "all that, all the time"—God. And if it is true that you and I are looking good, it is because of God, not us alone. It is God's abilities given to us, His materials, His energy—all of it. Anytime we're taking the credit for looking good, we'd be well advised to take a humbling deep breath and realize that at best we're co-creators based on Thy Will being done.

Let's humbly ask God to remove all that we would let get in the way of our growth. Thy Will shall be done, regardless of how we look. Amen.

So Breathe It.

August 3
GOING DEEP

When I was a boy, playing football in the backyard was one of my favorite things to do. During the huddle when the quarterback would tell me to *go deep*, this meant that I'd be going for a touchdown. Before the ball was put in play, my heart would start racing, and I'd most definitely be holding my breath until I was off and running for the end zone.

Today *going deep* has a completely different meaning. The glory of making a touchdown resonates with the glory of a successful spiritual quest within. The end zone, or my inner center, is where I get to during prayer, meditation, and, for that matter, anytime I need to hear the cheering of my Higher Power. The distractions of the outside world and the ones of my own mind can be seen as the opposing team, while making a touchdown represents me going spiritually deep within and staying there. Seeing my spiritual journey in the light of a game helps me to keep things light.

I am an innocent being playing on the playground of life. My playfulness contributes to the lives of everyone. The adult who continues to master the art of having fun and joy will never have the need of retirement.

So Breathe It.

August 4
POWER OF THE GROUP

It's often said that when one is not sure who, what, or where his or her Higher Power is, letting the group be it is OK. This might not be expressed in so many words, but several times I've gotten guidance for myself by either listening to or supporting someone in need. The form in which our help comes to us cannot be predicted. Closing our eyes, breathing, and just letting the energy of a group carry us is sometimes our best course of action.

When I watch my mind trying to figure things out, it looks like a hamster on a running wheel in a cage. That is, going nowhere fast. Noticing what my mind is doing is usually the first step. Taking a breath and shifting my attention to someone else's problems in the group can be just what the doctor ordered for my own healing. The power of identifying with another's hurt and pain has miraculous healing properties for all involved. To give and receive are indeed one in truth.

We've all heard it takes a community to raise a child. It is also true that in a trusted community, we too can be raised out of what ails us by God's helping hands.

So Breathe It.

August 5
CRUNCHING THE NUMBERS

There can be no doubt that the Universe is made up of an infinite number of mathematical equations. This includes our bodies as well. When we "crunch the numbers," whether it's with respect to diet, exercise, or how full and regular our breathing is, we will be affected by the precise laws of physics. However, the question remains unprovable as to how our spirits, thoughts, and the will of God affect the physical plane. But there is evidence that "energy" or the nonphysical realm affects the physical, even if scientists are slow to come to any definitive conclusions.

It's safe to say that no human will ever demonstrate perfect health and fitness. Though when we consider numbers and equations, we are well advised to be very aware of many calculations, from calories, to energy expended during exercise, even to the value of regular increases in the fullness of our breathing/oxygen intake. Wellativity speaks to adding in more and more healthy adjustments, rather than focusing on the regrets of the past.

God, I forgive myself and others for the trespasses that have occurred. I do my best and leave the rest, so that I may have room to multiply Your good, healthy, and loving gifts. Amen.

So Breathe It.

August 6
WHICH WAY TO TURN

Who hasn't been at an intersection and not known which way to turn? In a vehicle, on foot, or even considering a life choice? Looking in our mind for the next right decision sometimes doesn't work; where do we go when asking a trusted person(s) just confuses us more? That's the point when pausing may work best. Breathing and letting go of trying to make the decision is usually wise. The minute we release our grip of "trying," spiritual help/vision then has the space to enter our minds. Another way of affirming this: I get out of the way and pray.

It helps me to have less stress in deciding things when I remember that one way or the other, God's Will shall be done, sooner or later. Regardless of the speed in which things are unfolding, we can rest assured that God can wait for us to ultimately get on the same page as Him/Her.

God, in this breath I remember all is in Divine order. At every corner in my life, I give thanks for the opportunity to grow more in faith and trust in You. In truth, I pray to remember our eternal connection. All else has been designed from Your love, for the best and highest good of all involved. Amen.

So Breathe It.

August 7
BEING VULNERABLE

There are many levels of vulnerability people face every day. Currently recovering from one of the worst storms on America's east coast, I'm painfully reminded that our survival, day-to-day, is incredibly fragile. I originally started this Daily Breath topic before Hurricane Sandy hit. My intention was to elaborate more on mental and emotional vulnerability, but after my girlfriend had to remind me to breathe on more than one occasion, I've decided to change the tempo of this Daily Breath to focus on dealing with our being at the mercy of Earth's weather.

Dear God, thank You for all that I have and do not have. Although the world around me looks bleak at times, I'm grateful that I'm reminded to breathe in faith and hope for all in all. I know I can't know Your plan, but You've shown me how to trust the process, even when it's extremely trying. Thank You for also teaching me that You never abandon any of us, from birth all the way into the beyond. May I always remember that loss, difficulty, and pain are part of our growing into more loving beings of light. Amen.

So Breathe It.

August 8
OBSESSING

Being obsessive or obsessing over things doesn't necessarily mean you have a disorder. Everybody has obsessed at one point or another. Being aware that we're in that state of mind can make all the difference. Once we've realized this, taking a full breath will go far in helping to loosen the grip of oppressive tunnel vision. We're not talking about the focus needed for an important task, just the things that don't need as much attention as we might give them out of fear and worry.

The opposite of obsessing could be seen as not giving enough appropriate attention to something that warrants more focus. A good example of this is noticing we're not paying enough attention while driving. Rather than obsessing about what could have happened, why not just breathe a sigh of relief and find the needed middle ground?

There is no more perfect antidote to being obsessive than saying, and meaning, "Thy Will Be Done." In other words, turn it all over to the One who knows of your need before you do. Do it again, and again. Do it as many times as you feel you need to, to let go and let God.

So Breathe It.

August 9
CONVERSING WITH GOD

It's my belief that we all converse with God far more than we realize. To the extent that we can release our judgments and evaluations about what a conversation with God should look like, we are then free to include all of our thinking in a life-long interaction with our Creator. I know that when I'm anxious about what God may be hearing from my thoughts, it's time to take a breath and know that as I would understand a child of mine, and his or her way of being, so does God for me.

There is no question, statement, or feeling that God won't understand and lovingly accept. Coming from this place, we are then free to let it all hang out with our true best friend! The comfort we may experience with a human best friend is only a fragment of the unconditional love and acceptance we innately have with our source of life/the air we breathe, as is every thought we have. These are all made from the fabric of awareness freely given by the ultimate designer of thought!

Is there any thought more profound than one bred of love and gratitude?

Me: God, thank You, and I love You!
God: You're eternally welcome, and I love you just the way you are!

So Breathe It.

August 10
RELEASING THE VICTIM

There is nothing wrong with feeling like a victim of certain people, places, and things. However, easing the need, habit, or disposition of being a victim can be a big step in healing. When we take a conscious deep breath, we begin the easing or releasing process. Mind you, we're just easing the attachment or tight grip we may have on something, or something might have on us. We are not trying to change anyone or anything other than the overbearing feeling of victimization. We may indeed be a victim, but the point here is to get a few breaths in between the feelings. This may earn us a few precious moments to see our situation from a different/healthier perspective.

I can honestly say there have been several experiences in which I could say I was a victim. However, in the same truthful breath, I can also say if I had taken two or three conscious breaths before making a choice, in all probability I would probably not continue claiming to be a victim of myself or someone else's actions. Sometimes it does indeed take just one more moment or breath to alter lives in a healthier way.

In one moment, one breath, all of our choices in life have been finalized. Building a habit of taking one more moment and one more breath before acting can, in all probability, yield healthier outcomes.

So Breathe It.

August 11
EMERGENCY MODE

By definition, an emergency is a sudden, urgent, usually unexpected occurrence or occasion requiring immediate action. The one thing I've noticed that makes a huge difference in how I respond to an emergency is the level of resistance I'm experiencing to what is happening. Emotionally, it may be fear. Physically, it is constriction or tightness. These may all be appropriate reactions, but the sooner we can regain our balance or equilibrium, the better able we become to handle things effectively.

As you may guess, my first response in an emergency is to BREATHE. This keeps oxygen flowing to our brains, which enables better decision-making abilities. It also loosens the tightness being held in our muscles, which helps to maintain blood flow to the body parts needed for quick action.

It's been said you can't give what you don't already have. By taking care of our own safety/well-being (breathing), we become more able to help others in need. God helps those who help themselves. This is the starting point of all true public service.

So Breathe It.

August 12
RAGING AGING

How I've felt about aging has varied throughout my life. At this point I can say I usually have a new age-related sensation or discomfort almost every week; most definitely at least one a month. I very much can relate when people say getting older is a divine challenge to say the least. However, I've learned there's a fine line between acknowledging a true feeling or emotion and affirming the way it must always be.

My late stepmother, Jackie, taught me that when I notice I'm affirming and reaffirming something negative that I might be able to alter by changing my thinking, I should quickly say out loud "delete, delete." I always breathe easier when I catch myself unconsciously saying or doing something that I can change by being aware of it, especially when it has to do with aging. For example, when I find myself saying (out of anger or rage), "Youth is wasted on the young," it is a great help to say "Delete, DELETE," then BREATHE! As another one of my late mentors, Eric Butterworth, would wisely say when asked how old he was: "I'm as young as the morning, and as old as God."

It's OK to be angry, especially about aging. Yet don't stop there. Breathe, notice it's a passing feeling, and be youthfully creative in how you hold the inevitable human process of maturing.

So Breathe It.

August 13
MAKING THE BEST OF IT

Most of us have heard the saying that if you're given lemons, make lemonade! This is what's meant by making the best of it. Moaning, groaning, and complaining in our world doesn't do much good unless there's a goal and it's organized with others. For our day-to-day challenges, we'd fare well if we conditioned ourselves to make the best of things. This doesn't mean not to take safe and appropriate action but rather refers more to our consciousness or perception of the way things are.

If I'm uncomfortable with a situation or thing, I do my best to stop, breathe, acknowledge my unedited feelings, and ask my Higher Power for a more spiritual and loftier understanding of it. I might have to close my eyes, while taking a few more prayerful breaths. When I'm able to get myself out of the way, I'll almost always be given the deeper, more spiritual vision.

Dear God, I get myself out of the way, as I pray for a healing in my perception. I know it's not so much an asking of You, but rather a letting go, and a welcoming. Thank You for the ability to change how I see things, and for lemonade. Amen.

So Breathe It.

August 14
INNER TIME CLOCK

Aside from what I've learned from watching science and nature shows, my cats (Sobriety and Hope) have taught me how precise all of our inner time clocks are. They know to the minute when to start meowing for their breakfast. How this happens isn't as intriguing as the fact that we (all living beings) are deeply connected to the exactitude of our cycles. The inborn need to breathe in, and out, is one of the many cycles we cannot be separated from.

Time and space are real dimensions in the Universe. However, they are measured by humans. The rotation of our planet and its movement around the sun are what we are innately connected to, not the passage of digital seconds. When we turn our focus inward, breathe, and connect with our Higher Power, we become less attached to daylight saving time (DST) but are re-empowered by a spiritual light time (SLT).

We all got rhythm! Our cycles are precise. With respect to time, the only true adjustment comes in our perception. Is it possible that God really does have everything in Divine order/time?

So Breathe It.

August 15
CODEPENDENCY

A general therapeutic/recovery definition of codependency is that it is a desire to please others in unhealthy ways. That is, considering the wants of others more important than your own, usually at the expense of your well-being. The problem manifests itself as your need, which unfortunately bypasses the healthiest choice for all involved. As with all addictions, the first step involves the admission of powerlessness/unmanageability that the substance or behavior renders in your life.

We've all had points in our lives when we were caretakers to an unhealthy extent. Whether you are a declared codependent, or just noticing traits of codependency in yourself, breathing will assist you in staying in the moment of choice. Taking a few full breaths will *never* make things worse.

Working toward healthy relationships with other human beings is one of the highest challenges on our planet. It has been said that God speaks to us in and through all people. Conscious breathing will enable us to get the message being given to us in every situation. Liking it is, of course, optional.

So Breathe It.

August 16
HANDHELD DEVICES

Few would disagree with the statement that we're living in a time when most of us are looking down at our handheld devices probably more than is safe. As with all of our technological breakthroughs and gifts, finding a healthy balance can make the difference between being productive or destructive. Once again, awareness is key in each situation. For this Daily Breath, let's focus on the passage of time and our physical well-being.

What I've noticed is the wear and tear that happens on our hands, eyes, and necks when using/abusing our devices. When our hands or eyes get tired or sore, we should take that as a sign to stop, take a few breaths, and maybe connect within. Hanging our heads down for extensive periods of time can have some of the most destructive long-term effects on our body. When you notice this happening, consider changing your body position, rub and/or stretch your neck, and, of course, BREATHE. Getting into the habit of stopping, checking, and adjusting can make all the difference in the long run.

To be aware is to be alive. This philosophy holds true on most every level of our existence.

So Breathe It.

August 17
THE NEXT HIGHER THOUGHT

There's a spiritual/transformation game called The Next Higher Thought. The person picked to go first chooses a thought about anything. For instance, he or she says out loud, "The sky is blue." The next to go must voice a higher thought about the blue sky. For example, "The sky is blue because God created it that way." Then the first person must add an even higher thought, such as, "God's blue sky helps his children breathe air that helps them grow into more loving beings." And the game goes on as long as the players wish. There is no winner or loser, just the value that comes from challenging the other player to transform his or her thinking in enlightening ways.

The Daily Breath's version might sound something like this: The first player says, "I breathe." The second player says, "I consciously breathe because it helps me connect with my Higher Power." Then the first says, "By connecting within, I make healthier choices." And the second could state, "Through my conscious breathing and turning my Will over to God, I can live a healthier and more prosperous life." And so on . . .

Exercising the muscle of our perception is as valuable, if not more so, than exercising our bodies. When we let go of our ego's version of the way things are, there is room to be filled with the truth given to us from the Power within.

So Breathe It.

August 18
EXERCISE THEME: BALANCED VARIATION

It's hard to deny that most of us start exercising in order to maintain or to lose weight, not to mention the many other ego/fear-based reasons that drive us to be physically attractive. Perhaps these reasons motivate us as younger adults to get started with physical fitness habits. However, if not by our 40s, probably in our 50s and definitely by our 60s we see many of our fitness activities have taken a toll on the joints in our bodies.

My belief is that when we have a balanced wellness lifestyle, we do not need to go to extremes in exercise or eating/dieting. Very often I need to take several deep breaths when I see the over-the-top training that professionals are giving to all age groups. My motto is balance, consistency, and variation. I'll leave this huge subject with a recommendation for weight-lifting programs. Lighter weights are just as effective as too-heavy poundage if the exercise is done slowly and with an isometric pause during each repetition (see **wellativity.com** for more suggestions).

Most physical movement is best aligned with the rhythm of our breathing. During physical activity, having such words or thoughts in our minds as breathe, slow down, easy does it, focus, and listen to our body will almost always enhance our experience and provide a healthy and safe consciousness.

So Breathe It.

August 19
SHIFTING

OK, I'm willing to let go. Can there be a more healthy statement than that? When I say those words, and mean them, I put into action God's healing life in every cell of my body and mind. Yes, sometimes just a deep breath with the understanding that I shall resist no more what's best accomplishes a miraculous healing shift as well.

Let's take the opportunity at this very moment to shift our gears and take a healing breath. As we regularly practice this shifting, we get more and more proficient in opening to the healing life of the Universe. Automobiles have gears, shifting, and transmission built in. I believe human beings do too. In a car there's a clutch to release the gears. In people the "clutch" is our breathing. Our thinking is akin to the stick shift being put in the next appropriate position.

Shift/breathe, change stick position/change thinking. Breathe/change thinking. Driving takes practice; so does healthy living.

So Breathe It.

August 20
TAKE IT EASY

The phrase "take it easy" can fit just about anything we choose. One of the most common ways people use it is while saying goodbye to someone. When I read those three little words, it's second nature to relax my body as I breathe deeply. No matter how any of us use the statement, the common thread is one of letting go, a letting go of making situations more difficult or harder than they need to be.

In my prayer time, or even while I'm trying to figure out the best solution to a challenge, it helps to say out loud (or to myself) "Thy Will Be Done" and to remember that in the end, it's going to go God's way, no matter how I bring myself to any given experience. So it is in my best interest to take it easy as I let go and let God run the show; to breathe while I pray for serenity, courage, and wisdom. Amen.

The 11th commandment states: Thou shall lighten up! Another way of saying the same thing is: In my release, I find my peace.

So Breathe It.

August 21
WEATHER OR NOT

We're living in a time when the weather is more unpredictable than ever, not to mention the extreme effects it's having on every continent. Sickness, war, and weather rank among the most difficult subjects to bring up when talking about the Will of God or about everything being in Divine order. When one of the above has adversely affected someone we care for, good breathing habits may not do much for the hurt and pain, but it sure can help to slow down our immediate need to contract and resist during a given situation.

The one thing I've noticed the weather does for me (often to my initial dismay) is to loosen my attachment to material things. Furthermore, it helps me remember that there are very few guarantees in life. Whether we like it or not, the weather is helping us not only live in the moment but be grateful for all that we have and do not have.

There's no storm in our lives, or on the planet, that has not come to pass. If you're reading this passage, you have successfully weathered every climate condition. Congratulations on your impeccable batting average!

So Breathe It.

August 22
REAL INSURANCE

In today's society we have or can acquire insurance for almost anything. Yet, as many people find out, having insurance doesn't always mean they'll collect, due to the loopholes written into some contracts. If going over an insurance contract doesn't make you take several conscious breaths, you've passed most of us mortals on the evolutionary scale.

For the ones who are more spiritually inclined or focused, it's easy to understand where our real insurance comes from. We all have experienced and will experience substantial material losses. However, knowing the truth of our souls and spirits can anchor us in this ever-changing world of give and take. Nothing of this world has, does, or ever will adversely touch my soul. God created me, and God never fails. During my times of prayer/meditation I relax into my breathing as I affirm those words.

We're in good hands when we live in the assurance that God's love guides and protects us, now, and forever more.

So Breathe It.

August 23
COURAGE

It takes the highest level of courage to adjust the negative aspects of our behaviors. It is believed that these acts of courage are done without fear. I couldn't disagree more. When God's Will is at hand and I'm attempting to do the next right thing, feeling fear in my gut, I breathe. This helps to loosen the potential paralysis of fear.

As I breathe deeply, I make my safe, timely, and appropriate leap into the void of the unknown. Whether it's a business meeting or skydiving, it will take the same stuff that expedites acts of courage. Proper management of our thoughts and emotions will yield the internal fortitude we will need.

I am not this fear (breathe). I'm having fear. This fear as with all my emotions has a message. When I breathe into my feelings, I can see and hear the guidance better.

So Breathe It.

August 24
GRAVITY

It's my belief that gravity is one of the most misunderstood God-given blessings in our universe. Often we see it as a burden, an obstacle, and an unpleasant force that contributes to aging. What if we chose to see gravity differently?

Obviously, without gravity we, along with everything else (including Earth), would be lost in space. In addition, our bones, muscles, and digestive tracks very much depend on gravity for optimal functioning. When I realize the full importance of this gift, it's easy for me to take many grateful breaths of oxygen, which also depends on Earth's gravitational pull to stay in the atmosphere. Can we find anything that better demonstrates God's omnipotence and omnipresence in the world? Thank You, God.

As with the most basic laws that govern the physical universe, the spiritual realm is so governed as well. God, like gravity, Your love keeps all of Your children tethered to You. No matter how much we might try to defy our connection to You, Your golden string of light and love gives us the means to find our way back to You . . . always and in all ways. Amen.

So Breathe It.

August 25
THIS IS IT

"This is it" can be a powerful affirmation toward living in the moment. In reality, this specific moment in time *is it*, or, put differently, this moment is the only moment that will ever be. And, even better stated, **now** is the only time there is. I think it's beneficial to stop and breathe into the concept of "This is it!"

This world presents us with an unending supply of extreme activities to bring our beings into the experience of having no other time, or place, other than right here, right now! Communion with the essence of life, or God, with no distractions, is what we reach for when we do things that force all our thoughts out of our minds. This leaves us with the incredible lightness of just being, here, and now.

Thank You, God, for, the ever-present eternal moment of now. This sacred place is where we can and will always find You. This knowledge not only helps us to breathe easier but to be eternally grateful for Your infinite stream of gifts and blessings. Thank You, God, now, and forever more. Amen.

So Breathe It.

August 26
ADDICTION

By definition, to be addicted is to be enslaved by a habit or practice or to something that is psychologically or physically habit-forming. When looking at our habits or addictions (all humans have several), it takes a high level of integrity to determine what is healthy and what is not. To admit our powerlessness over something, as stated in the first step of the twelve steps, is not as bad as it might seem. I admit I'm powerless over the compulsion or habit to brush my teeth at least once or twice a day. For me, the degree that a practice makes my life manageable or unmanageable is at the heart of a healthy or unhealthy addiction.

It has become my habit (due to much practice) to notice when I'm contracting and/or not breathing well. Even in the midst of an unhealthy habitual action, my healthier breathing practice can and often does give me a priceless moment to pause for reflection on the next right action to take.

The power of the pause can be life altering. A moment, or more, of pausing before we act can be the time and space needed for our Higher Power to come to the rescue.

So Breathe It.

August 27
RIDE THE HORSE IN THE DIRECTION IT'S GOING

This is one of my all-time favorite aphorisms; none better exemplifies letting go and letting God take over and ultimately breathing easier. To give a perfect example, when I was a boy while I was horseback riding in upstate New York with my best friends, we would often take a path that our horses knew well and would trustingly follow unless led off it deliberately. The appropriate analogy is that the riding path was the same as God's Will for my life, and my guiding the horse was my willfulness or willingness.

There's also a similar saying: "If it's easy for me, it's right for me." Taken to the extreme, this can enable laziness. However, while in a planning phase, we may notice that we might be trying to force things. That's the time to breathe, to ask ourselves what the path of least resistance is. That path would most certainly be the one going in the right direction.

When we trust that the Will of God in any circumstance is best for us, we get to the level of consciously choosing it to happen. This is the essence of being a co-creator. I like to see God as a driver's education teacher who also has a steering wheel and a brake just in case.

So Breathe It.

August 28
ALL JOBS INCLUDED

Any job is as profound and meaningful, or menial and degrading, as we make it. Whether our job is voluntary or paid has no bearing on the value we are free to give it. Work is work is work. It is a task we are doing that is in our path to be done. As with most things we are free to choose to focus on, our thoughts about the jobs we have are 10 percent up to us.

I often go into my work day with the decision to look at my work in a different way. What I'll be doing in any given day may not vary much, but when I remember I have a choice to see it in a higher, lighter, and more gracious way, the sky's the limit. I might close my eyes, breathe, and acknowledge my habitual thoughts about my work; then ask myself: "is there another way to see my world today?" Usually I can breathe out a releasing "ABSOLUTELY!"

God, if indeed You know all, and I believe You do, then I know You know the next healthier, higher, and brighter thought I'm able to wrap my mind around. My prayer now is one of preparation and willingness. I'm now ready to step up to a new vista. Thank You, God. Amen.

So Breathe It.

August 29
GOD, HELP ME

I've been taught to understand that God/my Higher Power speaks and acts through all beings that I'm aware of. This doesn't mean I like or agree with what is being shown to me. God could be telling me not to do something through a mean-intentioned person. The point is to get in, and stay in, the consciousness of God's ever-present guidance and support. Often I'm not clear on the next right action, but as I pause to breathe, I can be certain that help is always there when I'm ready, willing, and able to receive it.

I've learned that so many of my difficulties in life are of my own doing, or not doing. I see so many people crying out for help (including myself at times) for things to be changed, when the tools to make improvements are closer to us than we can imagine. So I ask myself, why do we scream for God to do things for us that we are fully capable of accomplishing ourselves? Our prayers may be more effective if we were to say: "God, help me to remember, and feel, that I am fully able to do the next right thing in the direction of true health and happiness. Amen."

I believe we have been, are being, and will continue to be carried through our journeys. Even our greatest of prophets was not abandoned when He was breathing his last breaths.

So Breathe It.

August 30
THE POWER OF WE

The first word in the 12-Step programs, Wellativity's Twelve Principles, and the Constitution of the United States is "We." The significance of "we" as the first word in all of the above, and many others, is not only intentional but necessary for optimal effectiveness. The use of our highest knowledge, advances in technology, and extreme acts of human benevolence may have been actualized in the end by one person, but *ALL* were enabled because of many.

We are all breathing, thinking, and living on this planet together. We need each other for so much. We can't and won't get through this life alone. In reality, we are all one. In the most profound sense, we either all make it, or none of us will. Anything fun and meaningful has always been more enjoyable when shared with others.

Today, let's meditate and pray on the Power of the We. We can and will heal all, in all, sooner, or later. But We will do it together. God, We thank You for the way of Your creation. Amen.

So Breathe It.

August 31
LOST DATA

In this age of computers, most of us have had to deal with losing data or information. The reasons are rarely important in comparison to the stress of being powerless over our loss. In the past I've been told to breathe while seeing if there'd be a way to recover what may be lost forever. When I was calm enough, I'd breathe into the thought: what's the lesson here? Although I don't always get the answer, at least by asking the question, I believe the Universe/God knows that I'm consciously willing to learn rather than stay in regret.

Whether it's our own, or a machine's memory, not having them function properly can have the best of us holding our breath. Knowing there is no one right or perfect way of getting the information we want or need, we enable the many pathways to remain open by remaining open.

Memory, what a gift! As with any form of prosperity, we've been shown that when we give thanks for what little or much that we have, we'll activate the law of supply. Which in essence, is gratitude. God, thank You for all that I have, and do not have. Amen.

So Breathe It.

September 1
ONLINE

When we're in front of our computers and connected to the Internet, we are susceptible to far more than what appears on the screen. Put simply, triggers. When we are viewing subjects that are geared toward eliciting mental, physical, and emotional responses, it would serve us well to be on guard, at the very least. One of the best initial things to do when giving care and protection toward ourselves is to breathe. And, yes, continue breathing in a way that supports our highest health and safety.

The world being quite literally at our fingertips, we now more than ever would be wise to respect the ease of access to all the good (healthy), bad (unhealthy), and indifferent things that our world has to offer. When we connect with our Higher Power during prayer and/or meditation, we rally this benevolent Force to work through us. In this presence, we can rest assured that we are being guided and protected.

When we do the actions of welcoming our guardian angel(s) into our life and affairs, there truly is nothing to fear. Where we have shined the light, it is impossible to accommodate darkness. Amen.

So Breathe It.

September 2
STACKING THE DECK

With regard to our health, happiness, and longevity, I'm sure we can all agree that there are no guarantees. People ask me why I pay so much attention to my health and well-being. They often add: "After all, we're going to age and die anyway; you can't change your genes, not to mention the unpredictable events of the outside world." I might respond: "You're quite right, but I like to stack the deck in my favor." They will usually take a mystified deep breath and say: "OK, Scott, what do you mean?" Two basic things are implied by that statement. First and foremost, easier and enhanced mobility. Second, I enjoy being in my body more when I take better care of it.

It doesn't matter much to me whether there is one day or seventy years more to my life when I consider making my health and well-being my number one priority. In conversation, I hear most people agree with that, but I need to breathe my own mystified breath when I see how often some of us drop out what is most valuable.

I thank You, God, for designing our bodies to be on the side of healing and restoration. I pray that I may show my appreciation of this gift by taking care of my body, which You've temporarily given to me. Amen.

So Breathe It.

September 3
WHAT'S BEST IN US

To get right to the point, God, who I believe lives in all humans, is indeed what is best in us. True, each of us has a different ability in utilizing our God-like qualities, but we're all created to be able to come from a Godly place. Kindness, compassion, loyalty, and honesty are qualities I like to align my breathing with during my prayer and meditation times. This practice helps to kindle and rekindle those energies, which, in turn, attracts them back to us.

The Course in Miracles says: "To give and to receive are one in truth." Daytop Village says: "What goes around comes around." The Ten Commandments state: "Do unto others as you would have them do unto you." When held in this cyclical principle, being selfless or unselfish in giving out what's best in us can be done in a positive self-serving way.

Namaste: The divinity in me salutes the divinity in you! Isn't God just being God in, around, and through all of us? The work is to sensitize our humanness to the all-ness within all of us.

So Breathe It.

September 4
THE END

Whether in a movie, a life, or an experience, endings are usually packed with emotions for human beings. I'm learning to breathe into them, rather than run from or resist my emotions. When feelings of hurt, sadness, pain, or powerlessness appear in our lives, first and foremost, breathe. I then do my best to notice my judgments and evaluations surrounding them. As enlightened or God-centered as I might think I am, I'm still human and have less-than-holy thoughts about most every experience.

The ease of transition from one event, experience, or emotion to another is what dealing with endings is about. In a car we call this process its transmission system, going from one gear to another. To disengage the engine, a clutch mechanism must be used to make the shift. For us, our clutch can be seen as different ways to enable smooth change. Conscious breathing or thoughts of God and/or new things to come are some of the ways to help us let go and welcome endings as a necessary part of our lives.

The breath I'm breathing now has a beginning, a middle, and an end.
Everything, EVERYTHING we will think, feel, and do will also have its time.
When we truly let go and let God, beginnings and endings are easier to deal with.

So Breathe It.

September 5
HAPPY NEW YOU!

Every New Year's Day, the late Eric Butterworth would say "Happy New You!" He indicated that wishing ourselves a "happy new you" was a way of reinventing ourselves. It was obvious that a new year was upon us, but being coached to inspire a newness of being is what I believe he had in mind; this was meant for every day of the oncoming year.

All of us have had major changes in life during which we've needed to bring ourselves to each day in a new way. When we look closer at our moment-to-moment way of being, the fact is that this moment is as new as 12:00 a.m. on New Year's Day! Moreover, the breath you're breathing right now is also brand new! Last, but not least, the thought you're thinking this moment has never been thought in the place and time you're thinking it. The rhetorical question for us becomes: Are we bringing our consciousness to this moment, in an authentic and new way?

Making each moment new is not so much in the "doing," but in the "being." In other words, the newness of the eternal moment we exist in lives primarily in our perception. How can we ever really not be here now?

So Breathe It.

September 6
THE NETWORK

We live in a world, not to mention a universe, of countless networks. I believe a common universal thread of what entails a network is communications. Once we do our part in connecting with God/our Higher Power, we then have the potential of infinite networking. Most often we can do this through prayer and meditation. However, a portal in getting connected can be opened in communing with nature, our families, our breathing, music, writings, etc.

We have little or no true effective power alone. To have a successful career or business is to utilize the art of networking. In addition, to maximize our mental, physical, and spiritual health, we must also be able to establish connectivity with many avenues. One of the benefits to working with the 12 Steps or the 12 Principles is clearing the obstructions that may inhibit our access to many of our possible avenues. Indeed, the true benefit of making amends is a clearing.

Restoration of any relations, due to damage we may have been involved with, is at the heart of networking.

So Breathe It.

September 7
WHY PRAY?

It has been said that our thoughts are prayers. Yes, there are many, many types and methods of praying, but why do we formally pray? If you're into conventional religious practices or common spirituality, the intended result is basically the same—to communicate with our Source of Life, or as some might say, God. So if we go on the basis that the all-knowing Universal Power already knows what we have need of, why even make the attempt at talking to or asking for anything from the One?

As always, I try to keep it as simple as possible. The answer for me is alignment. When I pray "Thy Will Be Done," it's not that I'm agreeing with it, or getting some inside knowledge on it, but simply saying: OK, God, I'm willing to surrender my lesser or smaller willfulness and use my prayer time to get on the same page as you. Sometimes it can take 5 or 10 deep breaths before I can even get the words "Thy Will Be Done" out of my mouth.

When we get a wheel alignment in a car, does it not have a positive effect on the complete safety and comfort of driving? Can't praying be seen in much the same light when considering our journey through life?

So Breathe It.

September 8
SHARE FROM THE GUT

The intent to share from the gut, or from the deepest, most real place within us, may not be so easy. I find that our fear-based thinking minds are not comfortable with connecting with a source other than itself. I'm not sure why this is, but I do know that practicing communicating from our "center" or "inner source of wisdom" gets easier and more effective as we consistently work at it.

Without invalidating the information our brains have, it can be most advantageous to breathe, pause, and allow an integration of other communications to get into our awareness. It takes an evolved committee in our minds to permit other sources of wisdom, knowledge, and experience into a given situation. Again, briefly focusing on our breathing can gain us priceless moments toward safe and life-affirming actions.

Christ said, "Be still and know that I am God." I believe we of today can wrap our minds more comfortably around saying, "Be still and know that I am OF God." Amen.

So Breathe It.

September 9
THE RIDE

I once read in a popular book about a spiritual master who would sit by a river and listen for hours. He said the river would speak to him if he could get his smaller thinking mind out of the way. I often remember the concept he was referring to when I'm in nature, on a train, or even on a busy city street. Sometimes it's a loud and clear message, but if I take the time to listen, no matter where I am, I can find beneficial communications from within all people, places, and things.

Most of this book has been written during my ride on the train that travels along New York's Hudson River. You might not think the 5:01 a.m. train into NYC would be a spiritual time/experience, but I think it's the best time of the day to get spiritually connected. I can't tell you how many times I'd close my eyes, breathe, and listen to the train, and then let my writing come forth. If everything is God's creation, then could He/She not speak through any and or all of it?

The deeper and more quiet we become, the more there is to hear. It may or may not be in our language, but the One who is ceaseless in conversing with us most certainly knows what we are able to understand.

So Breathe It.

September 10
REMEMBER

Without a shadow of doubt, top on the list I've found to remember is that I am never alone. Yes, we may all go through times of deep loneliness, but that is quite different from truly being alone. Running a close second toward remembering is my breathing. "God, I know You are always with me." This is easily coupled with my inhales and exhales. To repeat this, or many other affirmations like this, can be incredibly uplifting in tough and not so tough times.

One of the most beneficial things in remembering what's most important to us is forgetting, often referred to as our "forgettery." There are always things to best remember with regard to our safety and well-being, but don't we all have a list of things best forgotten? Whether it's past hurts, resentments, and/or anything that's not serving our well-being to keep rehashing, let's do our best, and leave the rest.

Our minds can be seen as the most powerful of tools given to us. What we decide to relive, reenact, or just continually remember is best to be consciously chosen.

So Breathe It.

September 11
WHEN YES MEANS NO

When we say "yes" to life-affirming things, are we not saying "no" to the stuff that could take away from our health and well-being? Saying yes to a more charitable, benevolent, and forgiving thought or action is also a way of saying no. Here, no means we will not default to the fear-based negativity the world often shows us. The question becomes, what am I saying yes to in this moment? Sometimes taking a few breaths and then asking that question on a deeper, more spiritual level can automatically shift our thinking.

Some of us are more challenged than others when it comes to saying no to people, places, and things. If this comes up for you, it might help to remember the power of what your yes or no means. A prayer to remember this God-given ability is usually a good idea. Instead of begging God for the wisdom and strength, why not have it be an affirmative prayer that honors what He has already freely bestowed upon you?

God, thank You. Thank You for the freedom to choose yes or no. I'm grateful that no matter what I choose, You always leave the door open to come back to You to let You think, say, and do through me. For this, I give thanks. Amen.

So Breathe It.

September 12
WHEREVER I GO, THERE I AM

There are a great many spiritual, religious, and human ways of searching for ourselves. I personally have tried many of them and eventually came to the point of what I call ownership. I'm not sure when or why, but one day a person asked me who is it that had always been there through all of the good, bad, right, and wrong things in my life. The obvious answer was me! Like it or not, I've always been on the scene. Of course, breathing into this reality didn't always make it easier, just sometimes a bit less stressful.

Once we fully get we are right where we are, we can give up trying to find ourselves and focus on the Divine Presence/God within. It's my belief that He/She/It is much less judgmental about our shortcomings than we are. As with a transmission or reception, it doesn't matter why, it's just crucial that our location is exact, being who and where we are. Sometimes when I forget I remember a pin I used to wear that stated: "I've found myself . . . see, I'm right here!"

Once we discard our pretenses, masks, and fantasies of who we are, the truth of who we are is unavoidable. This becomes the truth that sets us free.

So Breathe It.

September 13
BALANCING THE IMBALANCE

A jet pilot knows that the vehicle is never going in a straight line or direction for very long. Constant adjustments are made to the wings in order to get back on course. Are we not much the same when it comes to navigating through our lives? Inevitably we're dealing with inner and outer unforeseen challenges, currents, and obstructions toward doing what our day has in store for us. Like the pilot, we make constant adjustments to stay on course.

If being God-centered is our ground of being, then using an effective navigation system is critical. As with all vehicles going on a trip, they must all function in harmony. This interconnectedness with our mission at hand is best kept intact with prayer, meditation, right action, and healthy breathing. Communication is the priority in all and with all safe, healthy, and fun journeys through life.

Each moment presents the opportunity for the pilot and co-pilot to work in unison. When we say "Thy Will Be Done," we are not so much giving up our job in piloting, but just the insistence of flying solo.

So Breathe It.

September 14
BEGINNINGS

As with endings, beginnings usually are packed with emotions. Fear of the unknown ranks among the top experiences for most. When I'm in the midst of this apprehension, I often remember the wise fact that fear is the same energy as excitement, minus faith. The best way to get back to trusting in an exciting new journey is to remember God. Breathing in the truth that our Creator is always guiding, protecting, and loving us through all, in all, always helps.

"In the beginning there was light, and He said this was good." I don't believe this biblical passage was meant solely for the story of Creation, but also for each new experience we find ourselves within. We humans have feelings surrounding everything we're involved with. As with the spectrum of colors in rainbows, the sun's/God's pure light is behind all the different hues. Without it, there would be no life at all.

We are filled and surrounded by the abundance of life. Being grateful for our life returns us to its source. If there is anything we need, let's remember this powerful affirmation/prayer: Gratitude is the law of supply. Thank You, God. Amen.

So Breathe It.

September 15
HOLY FITNESS

The first recollection I have of the word "holy" was while watching Batman on TV as a child. Robin, Batman's crime-fighting partner, would inevitably refer to an intense experience with a loud: "Holy . . . . Batman, what do we do now?" As a young viewer I thought nothing more of this than it was a way to shock me into the mystery of how to get through a dangerous event. As an adult, if I could have advised little Scotty, I would have told him Robin was raising his awareness to a God-centered place in order to better deal with things.

Today when I exercise I do my best to make it a holy experience. That means I pray before, during, and after working out. In the locker room, I'm consciously breathing while changing and thanking God for my health and fitness. While I'm in motion, I see it as a prayer as I invite God to move in and through me. Leaving the health club, I have prayerful/grateful thoughts for my willingness to have had a safe session in part due to my partnering with my holy trainer, God.

The essence of a holy communion may not be limited to a ritual on Sunday. The ritual of any work being done can qualify as a holy event, if we allow it to be.

So Breathe It.

September 16
BEING DIFFERENT

One of the most common things I've experienced in recovery is that people say they always felt different, or separate, from everyone. Being different, as each of us is, is not so much the problem as are the feelings of rejection and inadequacy. At this point in my life when I'm experiencing these emotions, I ask myself, am I really being rejected? If so, I breathe deep and understand it's probably due to the fear living within others. If it lives as a reality only in me, which often happens, I ask God for help in changing my perception.

What a great world it would be if we all could celebrate our differences, rather than fearing them. In truth, we all come from the same source. We all experience fear, hurt, and pain in much the same way. Most of all, we all want to be loved and accepted for who and what we are. I pray the day is coming soon, and I have faith it will, that we'll move from fearing each other to enjoying our God-given union.

Dr. Martin Luther King had the dream that one day we'd all walk hand in hand. So many others had and still have this vision. In tribute to all of them, I affirm that it will come to be, in God's time.

So Breathe It.

September 17
NUMBERS GAME

There are many schools of thought that give spiritual significance to numbers. In this Daily Breath I'll show you how I use a few numbers to connect with the God of my understanding. For instance, I often play a handheld Yahtzee game. It's a simple dice game in which you play with the numbers one through six. In short, when each of the numbers comes up I'm quickly brought back to a spiritual place. The number one of course, represents God. Two is the love I share between myself and another. Three symbolizes universal love. Four represents strength (hence the base of a pyramid). Five is money or prosperity; six is infinite supply or abundance.

Staying in the consciousness of the above life-affirming qualities is the significance of using something fun to achieve this. Conscious breathing is always the desired common denominator toward remaining open and receptive. I recommend that you pick a game you play and creatively choose the basic aspects of it to raise your consciousness with God, prosperity, well-being, and joy. Breathing is the one requirement. The rest is up to you!

Where there are two or more gathered in my name, I shall be there.

So Breathe It.

September 18
THERE'S YOUR SIGN

There's a stand-up comic who makes light of the stereotypical redneck- or southerner's humorous idiosyncrasies. He finishes each joke with the statement: "There's your sign." I've found it valuable to bring a similar levity to noticing the signs we're all given toward behaving in certain habitual ways. It can be very easy to be harsh and judgmental with ourselves when we notice that we're not showing up in life to the best of our abilities. Even if it's something as simple as holding our breath.

I always have a choice as to how I react when I see the signs that healthy adjustments are best. For instance, I become aware that my abdominals are overly tight, and thus my breathing is restricted. Usually I'll take a restorative full breath, but sometimes I'll have a negative thought with regard to why I hold unnecessary tension in my body. When I ultimately allow my Higher Power into my mind, I might correct my thinking because he produces a comical scene (like the Three Stooges or the Marx Brothers), making a joke out of why I'm holding my breath. The effects of unhealthy habits may not be funny to us, but how often have we heard "laughter is the best medicine"?

Laugh and the whole game changes!

So Breathe It.

September 19
GROUNDING/RAISING

We all have chakras or energy centers in our bodies. From the base of our spine to the top of our heads, there are seven in total. The base chakra is associated with our primal needs. The highest or crown chakra deals with our highest or most spiritual functions. Without getting into much detail, our health and well-being are related to the amount and flow of these energies.

When I'm obsessing with food, lust, and any of my addictive needs, my energy is likely to need raising from the lower chakras. I've found that a very effective way to move or shift my energy/focus is through visualizing and breathing. As I breathe in I locate, accept, and embrace the abundance. As I exhale I visualize, in an unforced way, the valuable energies flowing up my spine to my higher mental and spiritual levels. As with any task, practice makes progress.

In prayer, I let go and let God restore my mind, body, and spirit to its right balance. I affirm with and from God, all is in Divine order. Amen.

So Breathe It.

September 20
PENNY WISE

The essence of the old saying "penny wise, dollar foolish" can also have great application toward our health and well-being. For example, do we focus a lot of attention on the number of calories in our food but fail to exercise regularly? Or, do some of us often talk negatively about ourselves and others but never miss going to church on Sunday? Do we use our coupons to save pennies but spend inappropriate dollars going to expensive restaurants?

Making regular adjustments with my breathing could be seen as penny wise. On a positive spin, "dollar smart" would be releasing unnecessary tension and maintaining a relaxed body. Yet another might be thanking God for a healthy body and later making sure to get some safe and appropriate exercise. Can you see where you can merge your pennies into well-earned dollars?

Compensation is valid. In other words, the small efforts we put toward being healthy will pay big dividends in the long run.

So Breathe It.

September 21
PREJUDGMENT

One day I was riding the train and happened to notice a young man with a large tattoo on his arm. I thought it said "I love [a girl's name]." I thought how silly it was to have that tattoo; he might break up with her. This was followed with another thought about how young people can be so foolish. However, on my next glance I saw that the tattoo read: *Love one another.* I then took a humbling breath.

I notice that when I go into situations with prejudgments/prejudices, almost always I'm tense and/or contracted on many levels. When I become aware that I'm in such a condition, it's time to turn over my character defect to God. He knows exactly what to do with it. I know that I'm releasing my need to be better than others when breathing comes easier. This is not to mention the resounding echo of my Higher Power's voice saying it's safe to love one another.

I'm ready, willing, and able to let go and let myself be the conduit of Universal Love. Amen.

So Breathe It.

September 22
DELETE, DELETE!

As mentioned in a previous reading, my late stepmother, Jackie, always insisted that I should say "delete, delete" after speaking negatively. This may sound Pollyannaish, but at the very least it got me to disrupt the flow of negative thinking and speaking. At best, saying "delete, delete" would make a difference in the amount of negativity I'd be giving out, which in turn would ultimately find its way back to me.

If you believe in the philosophy of what goes around comes around, you will most definitely see the value of stopping the stream of negative energy. It's not as important *when* we become aware of what we're generating as it is to break it as soon as possible. The most tangible way to accomplish this, of course, is to take a nice big life-affirming breath. Seeing things from a loftier perspective will come next if we make the effort.

Realizing that each of us makes a difference in the world is exceptional. Understanding that each thought, word, and deed contributes to the type of difference is exponential!

So Breathe It.

September 23
WHAT IF

Is there a better phrase that opens our minds to new possibilities than "what if"? Having a closed mind could be seen as one of the most unhealthy ways of being. What if you were to go through the rest of your day looking at the world in another way than you're used to? Maybe you would see new opportunities for yourself that you were not aware of. Mind you, being open does not necessarily mean having a positive attitude. It just enables you to let go of your mental filter to new, better, and different things in life.

What if you were to have a conscious breath? What if for the next hour or so you challenged yourself to have 5 or 6 conscious breaths? The gist here is residing in the question of possibilities as opposed to a more automated or unauthentic way of living life. After all, haven't the great inventors of the world lived in that fertile place of "what if"?

One of the greatest advantages we have as opposed to the animal kingdom is the ability to question our way of being, not to mention the capacity to make healthy and productive changes.

So Breathe It.

September 24
NO FEAR

Many times I've seen the phrase "No Fear" advertised on products. In my opinion, to ignore or try to deny the presence of fear can be hazardous. Listening to what it's telling us and appropriately responding is the best advice. If I were going to advertise a fear statement it would read, "Respect Fear."

When things happen around us that warrant an immediate fear-based response, there's usually little time or question in what to do. Feeling fear that's due to how we're processing things in our life may need a different response. Possibly this might be pausing to breathe, then asking ourselves what this feeling is telling us. Sometimes, if we have trouble letting go of the fear, sharing with a supportive friend would be wise. I often find that my ego or pride will attempt to convince me that I can handle things on my own. At that point I do my best to breathe as I turn my willfulness over to the care of God.

Principle Three: Made a choice to allow God within to help us lead healthy lives.

So Breathe It.

September 25
WANTING SOMETHING SO MUCH

Wanting nice things for ourselves is part of a healthy life. Wanting things so much that it jeopardizes our health and well-being calls for some adjustments. We could wisely apply any one of Wellativity's principles to being consumed by our excessive desires. However, Principle One has the greatest merit in this context. Of course becoming aware that an extreme desire for something is costing us dearly must come first. Then we can pause to breathe as we begin to open to help.

It's a rare moment if I can honestly say Thy Will Be Done, and mean it, when I'm consumed with wanting something real bad. More than being honest about what I'm obsessed with, trust is ultimately what's being called for. Trusting that God knows what we really want can not only bring us greater peace, but the space to breathe easier.

Principle One: "We declared that we needed help in healing our bodies, that our fitness was becoming very difficult to manage." Granted, this principle refers to our bodies and our fitness, but remember the stress of obsessions directly affects our overall wellness.

So Breathe It.

September 26
IT'S ALL HIS

All we see is His, or God's property. If you adhere to the belief that He is our Creator, then we too are His property as well. However, He created us to freely choose to live close to or far away from Him. We appear to be connected to or separated from God, but in reality, true separation cannot be possible if there is no spot where God is not. We can only perceive his absence, not create it. Creating a real gap in His creation defies the truth that He is all present. In other words, it's only in our perception that God is not here, right now.

I choose to affirm in this very breath that the God of my understanding breathes each breath with me. I also choose to believe that He rejoices when I acknowledge His presence. I feel there's no greater joy parents can have than for the first time to hear their child voluntarily say to them, "I love you." In God's (our parent's) plan, and on His stage, we are all his, now, and forevermore. Making or not making the conscious choice to love and accept our true parent is the only drama there is in His universe.

God is all, in all, in all ways, always. Amen.

So Breathe It.

September 27
THE DRIVE HOME

Who doesn't know what it's like to want to just get home after a long day? For many, the journey requires a drive during rush hour. I now deem it the "breathe hour." There are few times during the day where we can actively use most of the 12 Principles.

Keeping our driving safety as the main focus, this is a good time to review what worked and didn't work for us that day with regard to our health and well-being (Principle 10). If your car is set up for a hands-free telephone conversation, connecting with some supportive people can be time wisely spent. The calls could consist of: making a health-related appointment (Principle 9) or clearing with someone who we need to clean something up with (Principles 4, 6, 8, 9, and10). Maybe it's a time to just work on our conscious breathing as we remain in a prayerful place while co-piloting our drive home with God (Principles 11and12).

Wherever we are traveling to, God is guiding, protecting, loving, and comforting us. Thankfulness for His gifts will make all drives home smoother. Amen.

So Breathe It.

September 28
BIG LITTLE STEPS

When going in a healthy, right direction, little steps are really big ones. When trying to make adjustments to our health and well-being, it usually has taken much discomfort to get us to the point of willingness to change. For some reason we are wired to try most anything but what's honestly needed before we truly surrender. When we've consistently practiced conscious breathing and connecting with the God of our understanding during prayer, the duration of pain and discomfort we'll be willing to tolerate will naturally decrease.

When we consider the big picture of our life, praying or meditating one or more times in a day could be seen as just a little step. But done on a consistent regular basis, access to God's healing power will be more available in a BIG way.

Remember, every Daily Breath you read, every time you include God, and most of all each time you ask for help, you're developing the muscle needed to make bigger and BIGGER healthy adjustments in your life.

So Breathe It.

September 29
BE REAL

Being true to yourself is what's implied by saying "be real." I've found that what we call being honest is closely related to being real, but is quite different at times. For example, if we want to change our eating habits, what can be seen as honestly the best food for us, may indeed not be the best or "real" next step for us. When in the midst of making healthy choices, stopping, breathing, and asking yourself honestly what's real for my next right step would be wise.

In yet another context, sometimes I ask myself if I'm being pretentious or am I being real or who I really am in a given situation. This also can require a long pausing breath or two. If I'm not sure or am experiencing fear with regard to being real, I may prayerfully state to God: "I'm willing to be shown what's real for me here." Then I do my best to let go and let Him show me in his time, not mine.

Be true to thy self.

So Breathe It.

September 30
IS IT WORTH IT?

It would be difficult for me to estimate how many times I've asked myself, "Is it worth it?" Choosing food, using substances that are unhealthy, saying things that were not from a nice place, or acting out with an affliction are some of the front-runners. For this Daily Breath, let's focus on coming from anger.

It's taken many years for me to understand what my anger does in the world and, most important, in me. As with all reactions, they always follow the universal law of having consequences. The fallout from speaking or acting in anger has endless returns from the outer world. But the duration of what happens to my inner peace and connection with God can last for hours, or even days. Mustering up all of my consequential thinking, I breathe into the question: Is it worth it?

When I become still I understand that my feelings of anger are often covering deeper feelings of weakness or powerlessness. When I remember this, I'm more able to ask God for help from a humble place.

So Breathe It.

October 1
ACCEPTANCE IS THE KEY

Accepting things in a given situation doesn't necessarily mean omitting safe and healthy actions. However, coming to a place of accepting things as they are gives us the best chance of taking sane, rational, and compassionate next steps.

The signs of being in a non-accepting space are restricted breathing, tension in our neck and shoulders, and a general uneasiness. To summarize: we are resisting things as they are. It can be seen as if we were expending the energy of a force field around us. This way of being is extremely depleting on all levels. When we notice we're in this state, let's breathe as we affirm that our Higher Power is guiding and protecting us.

Turning our lives and our affairs over to the care of God requires complete trust, a trust that is held in the presence of immense courage.

So Breathe It.

October 2
WHAT'S IN ME

The essence of what's in me is in you too. What makes me a precious creation of God has the same qualification for all people in the world. When we honor and respect the sacred life within us, our differences become a banquet for all to enjoy.

Differences in beliefs and opinions are always challenges for us in maintaining our peaceful inner space. During disagreements let's do our best to stay grounded in what binds us together. While interacting in opposition, what if one were to say: "Let's pause for a breath. Can we agree to disagree for the time being?" Sometimes it may just take a few frictionless moments to see things from a compromising position of diplomacy.

If we let the One source of life mold our thinking, just maybe He can show us how to peacefully co-exist, possibly even help us to identify with how He resides equally with all His creations.

So Breathe It.

October 3
ROW THE BOAT

"If you row the boat, God will steer it." I interpret that to mean if I consistently do the work in my life, He will guide and provide for my life better than I could do by myself. However, God has designed us as willful beings who are able to forcefully proceed in directions that lead us into temptations that separate us from Him. Yes, in truth we can never be separated from God, but the template of our lives gives us the opportunities, at least in consciousness, to walk closer or farther away.

Today I breathe in the conscious choice to turn my life and affairs over to my Higher Power (the essence of Step and Principle 3). It is important to remember that turning our will over is not a once-and-for-all deal. As a matter of fact, it can be done in as many breaths as we have in a given day.

"Made a choice to allow God's Power within to help us live healthy lives" (Principle Three).

So Breathe It.

October 4
EXPECTATIONS

At the heart of most upsets are unfulfilled expectations, thwarted intentions, and/or undelivered communications. This being said, it's no wonder so many of us are in an upset so often. In coping with life and the abundance of things that don't go the way we'd like them to, good breathing habits become an essential part of living in a relatively peaceful place.

Expectations can be seen as premeditated resentments. I recommend we have one and only one expectation, this being that God is and will always be with us; most definitely closer to you and me than we can comprehend. That being the case, aside from having a releasing breath, my first action is to acknowledge the presence of my Higher Power when working through an upset.

God, these people, places, and things are not meeting my expectations. I now am willing to allow You to lift my perception to a place where we work together in my detaching from my expectations. Thank You. Amen.

So Breathe It.

October 5
SPIRITUALIZE THE GAME

Understanding that spirit lives within and behind all manifestations, to spiritualize any happening is to see from a spiritual perspective. For our purposes it means that the primary purpose of a chosen game is to increase our spiritual awareness. Of course winning can feel great, but when we are spiritualized, it is not the sole focus.

Example 1: In baseball, I step up to the plate ready to receive a pitch. I breathe, relax my body, and affirm that my Higher Power shall in-power me to swing or not. In my relaxed focused breathing, I completely turn over my needs to the Spirit within.

Example 2: Card games can challenge us to remember faith and trust. This means adhering to the belief that all is in Divine order, even the turn of every card. As they are shown to us, let's breathe as we let go of our emotional attachments to the outcome. This is a very spiritual act, which can help balance our inner and outer worlds.

Respectfully seeing the spirituality and humor in our activities can be fun and challenging. Laughter is magical. Laugh and the whole game changes.

So Breathe It.

October 6
UNCONDITIONAL KINDNESS

"Unconditional" means no matter who, what, where, or when. Identifying with others having similar challenges as you can help you toward being unconditionally kind, even when it's not easy. This definitely should include acting in a safe and respectful way to ourselves and others. As we breathe from the consciousness of being kind, it is easier to respond to our Higher Power's guidance when how to do kind things is shown to us.

Another way to make being kind less of an effort is to remember what we give out, in one form or another, eventually comes back to us. In our meditative moments, let's breathe as we generate the energy of first kindness toward ourselves, then out into our world.

Fundamental to kindness is charitable thinking. When we see mean-spirited people, remembering that their disability is not being able to access kindness, use the same energy as understanding the plight of one who is physically disabled.

So Breathe It.

October 7
THE LORD'S PRAYER

Traditional Version:
Our Father, Who art in heaven,
Hallowed be Thy Name.
Thy Kingdom come,
Thy will be done,
on earth as it is in heaven.
Give us this day our daily bread,
and forgive us our trespasses,
as we forgive those who trespass against us;
and lead us not into temptation,
but deliver us from evil.
For Thine is the kingdom, and the power, and the glory
Forever and ever. Amen.

Wellativity's Version:
Our Creator, Who art here and now,
We gratefully acknowledge you.
Thy Kingdom of love,
Thy will be done, in our lives as it is through the Universe.
Thank You, God, for this day in which we breathe.
As we forgive our trespasses, and those who trespass
against us,
we open to Your unconditional love;
And we do not head to temptation, and in turn are delivered
from evil.
For Thine is the power and the glory forever and ever.
Amen.

*The times and words may change, but the essence of the
prayer is eternal.*

So Breathe It.

October 8
PRESENCE

My spiritual conditioning has taught me to regularly ask myself if I'm practicing the presence or absence of God. If we believe that God is in all points of time and space, then why do we so often think, talk, and act to the contrary? I notice that when I don't like what is happening in life it's easy for me to forget that there is a Divine plan taking place all the time, everywhere.

As painful and uncomfortable as things get sometimes, let's reach for the trust that He knows what's best. In each breath, know that God is here, right now, no matter what it looks or feels like. We never have to summon His presence, only open our minds to remember that His will is being done. When we affirm this truth for ourselves and others, we are practicing the presence.

We very much give the best help for others when we stand strong in our thoughts and actions that testify that God is not only here but available for us all the time. Speaking this truth can and does set us free, if we believe it.

So Breathe It.

October 9
INVENTING GOD

Each of us has a unique connection to and understanding of God. This means only you know how to connect with Him. Different practices may help to prepare you for your contact, but opening your mind and heart in your way, which God knows, must be authentically invoked by you each time you wish to commune with Him. That means different thoughts, feelings, and outer distractions must be dealt with in order for you to communicate with the God of your understanding.

There are a few things that Wellativity recommends for you in order to make conscious contact with your Higher Power. In stillness or activity, becoming aware of your breathing often is a start. Then, while having a relaxed focus, you breathe into affirming that God is not only with you but already knows you are attempting to communicate. Also, know that He will speak from and within whatever your mind is thinking. It's your job to clear the judgments and evaluations your mind is having about what is being shown to you.

Greeting God, thanking Him, and sharing love create the fabric in which we can embrace and be embraced during our communion with God.

So Breathe It.

October 10
LOVE SONGS

Love songs have a way of affecting our deepest emotions. What a beautiful experience it can be. However, when we listen to the words in many love songs, they often pull the listener into a story that differs from unconditional spacious love for another. I have gotten to the point where hearing the codependency in most songs is unavoidable. I take a deep breath when I hear phrases like: "I can't live without you," "your love makes me complete," "your love is why I'm happy," etc.

One day a solution that would help me to listen in a more joyous and positive way dawned on me. Very simply, every time I hear a singer talking about his or her love for somebody else, I put God in its place. Then all the dependency statements not only become true and accurate, but healthy too. Indeed, I can't live without God's love. His is the only one I need; most definitely with it I am made complete. With this translation I can continue to have my inspirational breaths during some of my favorite songs.

Tune your soul radio to the songs the Creator is singing to you non-stop. He has an endless collection of songs written just for you.

So Breathe It.

October 11
LIVING BY EXAMPLE

Living by example is the most powerful way to inspire people to open to their own healing. Sometimes it's easy to be too hard on ourselves when we realize that living by example must include how we handle our own shortcomings. Countless times I've sighed through my breathing as I reminded myself that it's about progress, not perfection.

The time between when we notice we're in the midst of a defect of character and the point at which we return to a place of peaceful integrity is the barometer of progress. It's amazing how quickly we can come back to this place when we humbly ask for help from our Higher Power. There are few better times that demonstrate "living by example" as when we surrender our pride and ego in our asking for help when needed.

"Having had a deep transformation as the result of these Principles, we live by example, and unconditionally practice these truths to the best of our abilities throughout our lives." (Principle 12)

So Breathe It.

October 12
THE PREGNANT PAUSE

When a couple is expecting a baby, the woman's pregnant condition produces a type of pause from the normal routine they are used to. Healthy behaviors and actions have become their responsibility in the partnership with God in the creation of a new life. There is no greater honor and privilege a human being gets to have in life as we know it. Each and every choice the couple makes is magnified as a potential life-affirming decision. Moreover, these actions can be seen as direct statements to God, a way of saying thank-you for the opportunity to co-create life with Him.

The pressures put on the woman are not only mental and emotional but quite real in every breath she takes. The main breathing muscle, the diaphragm, does not have the space it once had. Every time the expectant mother practices conscious full breathing, she literally breathes life into her precious one. This also helps her to maintain a healthier body and mind for herself as well.

Prayer: Dear God, thank You for this divine opportunity to forge a new life with You. Let my every thought, action, and breath be one that supports the growth of Your love within me. Amen.

So Breathe It.

October 13
POWER PHOTOGRAPHY

The process of taking a picture with a camera is a wonderful metaphor to demonstrate spirituality. The background chosen for a photo is the same as our attitude in a given situation. The lighting (or acknowledgment of God) can make or break any picture/situation. Of course, focusing the lens, or the thoughts we choose to focus on, determines the clarity or truth; last but not least is the act of taking the picture. I'm sure if you were to ask any photographer how important breathing is at the moment the picture is taken, all would agree relaxed breathing plays a crucial role.

Surprisingly, at the moment of taking a picture, briefly holding one's breath can be an effective way of minimizing the movement of the camera. I believe there's an even better breathing technique photographers can utilize. It's timing the picture to be taken in that silent moment that happens when one is going from inhaling to exhaling. The added bonus for picture takers is that when looking at their pictures, they will remember the conscious breathing at the moment they captured their picture.

If you believe in the importance of breathing conditioning, then more and more let's practice conscious breathing in those moments we are prone to fondly remember.

So Breathe It.

October 14
GAME OF RECOVERY

One of the promises in the 12-Step anonymous programs is that you will no longer regret the past. It's common to hear many people sharing in the meetings that they are grateful for the opportunity to have learned and grown from even the most gruesome experiences. How we rebound or recover from our shortcomings, defects of character, and the challenges life gives us is really what being "spiritual" means.

A person who is rooted in deep spirituality doesn't regret missing an intended target for very long but rebounds from the experience by remembering to use the tools of breathing, connecting with his or her Higher Power, and thinking more about the blessings intrinsic to everything that happens to us. Among the most valuable things we gain with "games of recovery," is the lesson that the game is usually not very much fun or effective when played alone.

Going for our dreams is so much more pleasant knowing that if we fall short, we have a team to help us rebound for the next shot.

So Breathe It.

October 15
HUMANISH

Humanish is the name I've come up with to describe the language all humans comprehend. It never has words exclusive to a given dialect. It's an unspoken knowledge or understanding we share in any experience. Usually it involves one of our five senses, survival, or a shared goal. When considering the essence of communication, it helps us hone our listening when we become aware of the many languages that go beyond words and sentences.

I know I've been guided countless times by my Higher Power, my intuition, and my experience. How these communications come into my consciousness is through a knowing, or a feeling. When I become aware that a message is being extended to me, connecting with my breathing is almost always done before I attempt understanding or next right actions.

You shall know the truth and it will set you free. The truth can be expressed in words, yet to experience it fully we will have to let go of all descriptions.

So Breathe It.

October 16
IN GOD WE BREATHE...

"In God we trust" appears on our currency as an affirmation of our belief as to where the source of prosperity can be counted on. This is one of the most powerful affirmations we have. Going one step further, any statement or phrase that follows "In God . . ." will have utmost potency woven into it. How assuring it is to know and affirm: In God we breathe and have our being. When we let this truth permeate our consciousness, the fear that once produced stress no longer will carry the punch it had during the unacknowledged presence of our true parent. Sometimes I just let the affirmations flow through my mind and in my words as they come up.

Where God is, there is no fear.
Breathe.
God is in the air I breathe.
Breathe.
Thank You, God, for all that I have, and don't have.
Breathe.
All that I truly need I can find in this moment here.
Breathe.
In God we rest.

So Breathe It.

October 17
DIALOGUE WITH GOD

For the most part, conventional types of prayer are monologues presented to God. Not that this is wrong by any means, but what if we open to the concept that God is available for a two-way conversation, or, let's say, a prayerful dialogue? The perquisite to this would be that not only does God hear us but can and does respond in ways each of us is able to understand. Far beyond any leap in technology we've made to date, developing our two-way communication skills with the God of our understanding will outstretch any bridge built in our history.

I take a full and relaxed breath. "Hello, God." The thought comes into my mind, "Hello, Scott." In the next conscious breath, I hear myself saying: "God, I love You." In my heart and mind I know and feel the resounding communication: "I love you so very much too."

"I'm incredibly grateful for what You've given me, God."

"I know you are. Thank you for your trust, faith and courage to believe I'm here with you, now, and forevermore."

In unison we affirm: "Amen."

True prayer conditioning becomes more than reciting words. It becomes a practice of listening and responding with the One who gave us the ability to do so.

So Breathe It.

October 18
SECRETS OF LIFE

A few years after my mother had passed away, I vividly remember her coming to me in a dream. Her message was that she came to tell me the secrets of life. In my dream I was holding my breath in anticipation as we walked into a room in which the door closing would be the end of the dream. You can imagine my feelings of upset as I awakened to the vision of a closed door, with no secrets revealed. There is, however, a long-term payoff to this unforgettable encounter with my mother.

Over the years since the dream, each time I believed I learned something very important in life, I'd smile and take a deep breath as I would hear a voice telling me: "You see, there's another secret in life I said I'd share with you. Just not in the time you thought it would happen."

I'm smiling even now as the thoughts of the deeply embedded secrets in all of life's experiences are coming to mind, such as: Have patience and faith, let go of your expectations of how and when things should happen, trust the process, and, of course, always keep breathing.

In God's time, not mine, more shall be revealed.

So Breathe It.

October 19
MUSCLE OF CONNECTING

The developing of any ability, metaphorically speaking, can be related to strengthening a type of muscle. Given that each person has a unique combination of beliefs, feelings, and conditionings, their ways of connecting with a Higher Power, or the God of their understanding, needs to be cultivated through the twists and turns in life. As they mature, so may their understanding of the value of staying connected within.

In order to achieve significant lasting benefits when exercising our bodies, it must be done on a consistent and regular basis. One of the many payoffs to this is when certain situations demand our strength and endurance, our fitness will show up for us in unexpected ways. So each time we consciously breathe, become still, and welcome God into a given moment, this in turn is working out the muscle of connecting.

Acceptance of our capability of connecting with our Source of Life is paramount toward developing a deeper consistent bond. With each intentional thought of our God, we connect more and more moments of this Divine connection, which in reality has never been broken.

So Breathe It.

October 20
SLEEP PREPARATION

It's common knowledge that going to sleep angry or upset is not healthy for us. What we may not be so familiar with is the value of going a bit further in preparing ourselves mentally and emotionally for a better internal place of rest. Yes, prayer and meditation in general are among our best choices for the last things to do at the end of the day. However, for most of us it's not done all the time.

If there's something that needs resolution prior to going to sleep, and the relevant people or things are not available to accomplish this, it's a good idea to use some of the 12 Principles in clearing the way for a restful sleep. Following is a brief example of what it has looked like for me.

God, my reactions to so-and-so got out of control today, and I could have handled myself differently (Principles 1 and 4), breathe.
God, please help me to come to a place of peace for now; show me how to restore things back to a healthy and peaceful place (Principle 7), breathe.

Including God in as many ways as possible is what works best. In the beginning, and right through to the end of all our days, let's bring it all to Him.

So Breathe It.

October 21
WAKING UP

Here's a healthy game or challenge for you. Do your best to have your first conscious thought be of God. After that, creatively build your consciousness around your Higher Power's presence. This is not only a divine challenge but a very wise practice during the first minutes of your day. Even with a spiritually sound morning routine carried out, continuing to dialogue with the infinite Power within will strongly impact the rest of our day as well as the world around us.

"I'm in a rush to get to the train, God. You know if I stop to pray now, I'll miss the 5:01," I say to Him as if He doesn't already know the situation at hand.

"Are you breathing? Can you move quickly while having a relaxed body? Won't it be more rewarding to make it to the train knowing we accomplished it together? Including Me in the midst of hurrying will help you. Remember, I can and do work in mysterious ways, even when it comes to getting you safely on the train."

Conscious breathing helps us not only to stay connected to Spirit but also to effectively get the job at hand done, safely.

So Breathe It.

October 22
SWING YOUR SWING

Some of the best golfing advice I've ever heard was: "Swing your swing." I believe this means that one would be wise to be as natural as possible and not try to conform yourself into an ideal picture of how someone else thinks you should swing a golf club. This speaks to accepting ourselves the way we are and doing the best with what we're able to do right now with what we've got.

Of course when trying to effectively get a golf ball into a hole with as few swings as possible, we must conform to the laws of physics and all of the given variables. This is when trusted support is most helpful, someone who sees our assets and liabilities from a distance and then coaches us with attainable direction. Whether it's golf, dealing with life, or going for our dreams, breathing into a moment of complete self-acceptance is great advice when swinging our energy in any course of action.

God created you and me with unique qualities possessed by no other. Like the healthiest foods, we are much the same—best served natural and with as few additives as possible.

So Breathe It.

October 23
CONNECTING WITH ALL AS ONE

We must start from the truth that we are all one—one race, on one planet, with one Creator. Whether we're comfortable with how our brothers and sisters have acted, or what they believe in, the One who gave us life ultimately connects us. Questions have a wonderful potential of getting our thinking past our differences to an acknowledged common ground of coexistence.

Are we breathing the same air? Do we have similar safety and survival concerns? Is not loneliness cold and upsetting for all of us? What thoughts can I fill my mind with that will generate a compassionate peaceful energy? Can I focus on understanding you rather than being understood?

In each moment we have a choice, an opportunity to actively stand as one people, or not. God has given us all the freedom to choose peace or conflict, love or fear. In each moment we can breathe in the prayer of oneness. Doing that right now will make a difference to us all. Amen.

So Breathe It.

October 24
CONTEMPLATING LIFE

Contemplating life from the highest point of view is as close to seeing things from God's perspective as we can possibly achieve. To be seeing something from the highest point of view implies an accurate vision of the way things are. It's an even higher level to see things ultimately turning out for the benefit of all. When our beliefs, feelings, and evaluations work their way into our perception of an event, getting to that loftiest place becomes difficult at best.

It is an evolved soul that knows when and how it's coloring a circumstance. This is not something to judge ourselves for doing but to breathe into the awareness that we're doing it. In A Course in Miracles, one statement I use to loosen my insistence on seeing things my way is: There is another way of seeing the world.

To just be here now with nothing added is one of the greatest challenges. We will always have our judgments and evaluations of the way things are. Noticing them, releasing our attachment to them, and breathing are all part of just being here now.

So Breathe It.

October 25
OUR LOWER POWER

So much has been said about connecting with our Higher Power. I believe it's also of great importance to acknowledge our Lower Power and how it plays a critical part in our survival. Rather than viewing our Lower Power as bad or evil, why not see it as an essential aspect to our evolution toward becoming God-centered beings of light and love?

The brain stem, where are located basic primal functions, is in the middle and lower sections of our brains. If there is any imbalance of emotions, desires, and addiction issues, they will no doubt have some root in this area. If there was a "dark place" in our bodies that could use some intentional "lighting," this would be it. Practicing the habit of consciously breathing as you visualize God's light infiltrating your entire brain is time well spent.

Breathe in: "There is no spot"; breathe out: "Where God is not."

When we have the context of using our bodies as tools for enlightenment, growth, and service, all its functions are essential and holy.

So Breathe It.

October 26
RECOGNIZING OUR PATTERNS

Regardless of our feelings about how we see ourselves, our patterns or behaviors have gotten us to where we are. One of the spectacular qualities we have is the ability to co-create things with God. In order for us to create healthy and fun lives, we must first recognize habits or patterns that have gotten in the way. Principle One deals with acknowledging the difficulty of managing some of our unhealthy behaviors. In the moments of truthful admission of being powerless in these areas, a good number of deep breaths can be comforting.

During these needed breaths of comfort it might also help to remember this saying: Easy Does It. Coming to grips about the way things are for us is a blessed time. Not being pleased with how we've dealt with things can be enough to make healthy/safe adjustments. Beating ourselves up or being overly judgmental may just get in the way of God's waiting help.

Dear God, please help me to forgive myself for the trespasses I've made. In my own forgiveness, I'm sure to see the next right step toward safe and healthy restoration. Amen.

So Breathe It.

October 27
EVERY THOUGHT

A common belief in the world of recovery is that every thought brings us either closer or further away to acting out with an affliction. I believe that when this theory is applied to our spirituality, it is just as applicable. In other words, each of our thoughts brings us closer to the God of our understanding, or farther away. If we adhere to the belief that God is omnipresent, then in truth it is only a moving closer or farther in consciousness.

I'm saying "only" in consciousness, but let's not underestimate the importance of what we choose to fill our minds with. Everything you, or for that matter anyone, has intentionally created has originated in conscious thought. The great news is that what we choose to continually think about is one of the few things we have power over; one of the most powerful thoughts we can breathe into is the thought that God is working in and through us. Let's choose to remember this as often as possible.

There is nothing mere about what we hold near and dear. Indeed, there is nothing to fear, for God is here.

So Breathe It.

October 28
BREATHING BLITZ

In this day and age almost everything we consider good for us is made into an ultra, mega, or maximum form of sorts. Aside from breathing conditions that require medical assistance, in order to gain maximum results with our respiration we must intentionally make the effort. Achieving the results we want comes down to the intensity of our focus.

To blitz something is to go at it from many angles as intensely as possible. Reading *Wellativity's Daily Breath*, physical breathing exercises, affirmations, or having a conversation with someone on the importance of improved/conscious breathing are several ways to blitz the quality of your breathing. The great news is that right now you can reduce your stress levels, increase the vital oxygen content in your cells, and connect with your Spirit just by taking a few conscious deep breaths! Thank God for this ability. Amen.

We literally breathe in God's life with each breath. This is true mentally, physically, and spiritually. Our improved, conscious breathing impacts all of these domains. Awareness is more key than the technique. The bottom line is breathing works, always, ALWAYS.

So Breathe It.

October 29
SMALL PRAYERS

In my experience, the most heartfelt and effective prayers often come in the form of one word. It's true that all thoughts can be seen as a kind of praying, but for our purposes here let's look at the ones that help to consciously connect us with the God of our understanding.

"Hello" can be understated in its potent significance as a complete prayer to God in itself. Saying hello to God acknowledges His presence; our greeting is seen as a statement that He comprehends the friendly gesture. I've found that when I sit in the stillness and completeness of a simple hello to God, I often hear "Hello, Scott." Of course this is in my thinking, but who's to say He is or is not the one who's speaking back to me by generating the thinking in my mind?

Help, thank You, I love You, I know You know what I have need of, go with my loved ones, and all is in Divine order are the simplest of prayers that have the most meaning. Yet the one that God prays with me most often is: "BREATHE."

So Breathe It.

October 30
HURT AND PAIN

It's not a mystery that for every dimension of our beings there is a form of hurt and pain that can be experienced within it. No more is the multidimensional gift of breathing effectively used than in dealing with discomfort. From the labor of childbirth, to the searing tears of loss, to the shock of physical damage, being conditioned to use your breathing in order to bear things is one of our best tools we can intentionally develop.

Starting right now let's initiate a new level to our breathing conditioning programs. In the unlikelihood that you haven't already done so, have a conscious breath now. In addition, let's resolve to take a few deep breaths as soon as possible the next time we experience any hurt, pain, or discomfort. Starting with smaller discomforts such as hunger or pain from our shoes can be good practice for the larger hurts or pains which are sure to eventually come upon all of us.

All is not lost if we are breathing. Focusing on our current breath will certainly carry us to the next moment. Giving our minds and bodies an abundance of oxygen can always help with all current experiences.

So Breathe It.

October 31
BATTERIES INCLUDED

Our batteries are included! In fact, every cell in our bodies is charged and rechargeable to work 24 hours a day. Aside from an array of nutrients, every cell must be powered to assimilate these things in order to perform its functions. The oxygen we breathe is the common denominator needed for each cell in every body. The infinite cells in the human race can do without most of their required supplements for varying amounts of time, but oxygen (the main ingredient in water), tops the list of most important elements. Without it—well, let's just say that when you breathe your next breath you are literally giving life to the trillions of cells that make up the one life called you.

Our infinite battery and charger are one and the same. In this context "batteries included" not only is a given but one that has been designed for us to voluntarily include on a moment-to-moment basis. By consciously making the effort to be inclusive of our one true power source, we gain access to unlimited strength and endurance.

In our affirmation of our true Power Source, we can maximize our potentials. To be plugged in, or connected, is to be blessed.

So Breathe It.

November 1
IF GOD EXISTS

From Christ during his crucifixion, to the most pious clergyman, to the common worshiper, all have had moments during which their faith was weakened or temporarily nonexistent. We've all had experiences when we felt forsaken and betrayed by our Creator. If God really exists, then why must such pain, destruction, and loss be so? If you and I had His answer I honestly believe that (1), we wouldn't understand it; (2), we'd have extreme difficulty accepting His truth about it all.

Faith, trust, and hope are likened to spiritual muscles. To develop these qualities they must be exercised. In this quest for spiritual fitness we'd be well advised to breathe our way through each of our apparently insurmountable challenges. Let's breathe into the truth that we shall overcome, that we shall be reborn into a new life of faith. Most of all, we will see that we were never forsaken but carried while we needed to trudge through our test of darkened amnesia.

As every night has given way to the dawn, and each day must surrender to the dusk, all of our doubts will be blown away by His winds of inevitable change.

So Breathe It.

November 2
STANDING ON OUR OWN, NEVER ALONE

Many of us depend on others so much that we can have trouble when life calls for us to stand on our own. Why we've been overly dependent or codependent is not as important as understanding that when we're ready, God has supplied us with support that goes far beyond our comprehension. I just know that every time I've taken a stand, unforeseen help has shown up in ways I could never have predicted.

When we can let go of how life is supposed to look or work for us, it usually turns out better than we expected. Having had my share of overly needy personal and professional relationships, it has taken nothing less than unceasing prayer and right action to breathe my way into a healthy way with my interactions with others.

Let's not mistake passing feelings of loneliness for the unchangeable truth: We never were, never are, and never will be alone. Thank God.

So Breathe It.

November 3
INJUSTICE

When we trust that God's will is being done, how real is "injustice"? For some this question can imply that we should deny our feelings of injustice, the reality of crimes committed, and being treated unfairly. It comes down to a choice of how we will perceive events. As a matter of fact, when we hold our breath in the act of denying our feelings of injustice, this can prevent us from letting go and letting God heal our lives and perceptions.

So many times I've found myself turning my back on my feelings in the pursuit of being spiritual, or God-centered, that I was forced to relive certain experiences until I could fully accept myself and others; more often than not, true forgiveness was a barometer of a complete letting go and moving on.

How many times have we dealt with apparent injustices only to see there was a greater plan with unforeseen future blessings?

So Breathe It.

November 4
INTER-GOD-NET

The Internet offers us virtually instant access to unlimited people, places, and things. It's possible to imagine that we have a similar two-way access with God within all situations. We're not imagining this access to be solely informational. What if the possibility was that from any place in the universe, our potential was to access, or to be accessible to, unlimited power and wisdom? What if we're just in the process of being upgraded to a better "Inter-God-Net" accessibility?

This accessibility includes everything. That means power, wisdom, communications, prosperity, health, and protection. The primary requirement to access the Inter-God-Net is connectivity, or getting plugged in. Also one of the most essential principles is knowing our powerlessness, or unmanageability, when we are experiencing a "limited signal." Just as important as understanding what we are without our power is believing that His Net and its capabilities exist. When the right steps are taken, the Inter-God-Net is there for all.

He created a simple system for complicated people.

So Breathe It.

November 5
BEING HUMBLED

One of our most painful experiences can occur when we are brought to our knees in desperation, when all we've done appears to be ruined or broken. In those times I do my best to breathe in and say, "God is," and breathe out, whispering, "I am." In these times that affirmation has been often said with much struggle and many tears. However, being humbled down to my knees seems to be a place reserved for me when I let go and finally let God into my life in a way that I was resisting or fearing.

Fault, blame, and condemnation have no place in the space of true God-centered humility. When I notice them creeping in, as they so often do, I again and again breathe deep as I humbly ask my Higher Power to lift my defects. I do my best to make sure I am releasing them so they can be lifted.

Dear God, I pray in the hopes that I may let go of my resistance to trusting You. I know You patiently wait for my complete willingness to release unto You all that is bred from fear. Thank you. Amen.

So Breathe It.

November 6
BEING JUDGMENTAL

The way most of us have been brought up is with different variations of what's right, wrong, good, and bad. We were so conditioned to this that we didn't have a chance to choose or consider what was real for us. The end result for myself was not knowing when to stop being judgmental toward myself, as well as toward others. My first and longest-running lesson in a more loving, inclusive, and God-centered way of being is noticing when I'm being judgmental. I don't try to change it but rather to breathe into the awareness of what's going on in my mind.

What works for me is that after I'm aware of my critical response, I then have the opportunity to make the choice of turning a situation over to my Higher Power to cast judgment if needed. I then have more space not only to breathe but to consciously choose a more loving and forgiving way of being. Mind you, the next right healthy action(s) often will include remembering and letting go of the past.

I let God guide my life and affairs; in this way I can live peacefully remembering that the past is over, and it cannot hurt me.

So Breathe It.

November 7
REST AND RECOVER

We know that all mental and physical activity requires rest and recovery to some extent. After we exercise our bodies, minimizing activity allows the cells to regenerate and build new ones (most strength and endurance gains are made during sufficient rest periods). Most of us have noticed that with regard to our minds, it is rare to have them shut down completely. Quieting and/or slowing them down is more of an art than a skill. Of course conscious breathing not only works but also can be seen much like an artist rinsing his paint brush.

Our souls are directly connected to the eternal, inexhaustible Source of Life. One of the major benefits of creative quieting and slowing down is the In-Powering from God to our souls and ultimately through our minds and bodies. So in each relaxed breath, we are saying "yes" to life, through and through.

To allow rest and recovery is to enable improved communication. To be fully In-Powered is to be able to listen and respond to God's voice within.

So Breathe It.

November 8
DOWN SHIFTING

If you've driven a stick shift automobile you're probably aware of how valuable intentional downshifting is on a hill or before rounding a turn. It not only saves wear and tear on the brakes but can make the difference between skidding or not. In both scenarios timing is key.

During our human experiences the energy or speed at which we function can make the difference between success and failure in a given task. Obviously the consequences have extreme variations. When I honestly look at the times when I was making important decisions, almost invariably slowing down or down shifting my energy would have proven adventitious. It is nearly impossible not to decrease the velocity we're functioning at when we focus on our breathing. Mind you, moving fast is not innately wrong; it's just that listening and responding to communications is much more challenging.

EASY DOES IT.

So Breathe It.

November 9
THY WILL BE DONE

If you're one who sees the importance of what is meant by "Thy Will Be Done," you realize that God and His order of manifesting the universe is critical to the way we conduct ourselves. When we can release or surrender a limited way of thinking, it is clear that God's Will is being done, always, no matter what. Even allowing us to be willful beings, with all the consequences involved, may indeed be within what is God's Will on earth. That can be a tough one to wrap our minds around when looking closely at our volatile human history.

When I'm in prayer and I hear myself affirming "Thy Will Be Done," I remember to breathe as I know the truth of His divine order is already so. My affirming it helps to condition my heart and mind, and that's all it does. It loosens my expectations, needs, and wants. I believe the true purpose of prayer is to establish and help to maintain a God-centered consciousness, not change outcomes.

Thy Will be done.
I get out of the way and pray.
In my release is my peace.
Let go and let God.
Thy Will is done.

So Breathe It.

November 10
HEALTHY DISTANCE

In learning about codependency, keeping a healthy distance from some person, place, or thing is often referred to as respecting boundaries. I was brought up in a fairly large family, and honoring physical and emotional boundaries was a behavior hard to count on, let alone demonstrated by the ones who had little capacity to do so. This all may sound quite negative, but in order to heal in this area, we must acknowledge our truths. Melody Beattie in *The Language of Letting Go* has much to teach with regard to codependency.

With respect to breathing, is there anything more conducive to holding our breath than when we feel threatened by an intrusion on our boundaries, or healthy distances? I've found that remembering that NO (which Melody teaches is a complete sentence) could be said while I was holding my breath but was most always quickly followed up with a freeing full healing/releasing intake of air.

Whether it's yes, no, or maybe, in the end honoring a healthy distance helps us to breathe easier.

So Breathe It.

November 11
COME TO ME

It is we who must create Heaven on earth. Right where we are, right now. That means the energy of God and all His love and acceptance of us is indeed a heavenly condition for all, always. Thy Will is already done, on earth as it is in Heaven! God does not need our prayers for this to be so. He is eternally saying to you: "Come to me." Being omnipresent and omniscient, God does not need your prayer/permission/supplication to be where he already is.

We'd be well advised, in this very moment, to breathe in the truth that we need only give ourselves permission to let God into our consciousness; that's how we go to Him, not the other way around. What would this do for your breathing if you realized that in every moment God has been whispering to you, "Come to me, my beloved?"

There's nothing to be, do, or have in order to go to Him. Just an awakening to what is so.

So Breathe It.

November 12
STANDING ON MY OWN

As a young boy I was required to walk with a full-length leg brace and crutches. In addition I had a twin sister to lean or depend on for much. Just with these examples, you can see how "standing on my own" from early on was not made easy. Looking back into all of our pasts, I'm sure each of us has examples of how it was challenging to stand or live independently.

With so many mental, physical, and emotional needs we demand from life, it's no wonder that so many of us not only have difficulties breathing full and easy but are weary to trust in the provisions of an apparently unseen God. However, when each of us looks with the smallest bit of logic toward the events in our lives, it's obvious that we're given what we need to stand on our own. That includes being carried through times in order to be placed upright once again.

Yes, we've been In-Powered by the one and only true Power. It's our lot in life to learn to crawl, stand, balance, fall, get back up, balance, and walk on our own with appropriate support when needed.

So Breathe It.

November 13
THE CAVALRY

In this day and age people don't have a firsthand experience of the cavalry coming over the hill and saving them from attackers. In tandem with this thought, I remember when a wise man (Stewart Emery) was addressing a self-improvement group he was leading, and he said: "I have some bad news and some good news for you. The bad news is, the cavalry is not coming over the hills to save your butt. The good news is, there are no Indians!" Clearly Stewart was alluding to the fact that on an internal or spiritual level, our human conditioning to protect ourselves doesn't have the same application to the fears many people live in.

I get that I am my own cavalry and can be the Indians as well. It's my choice. What I think and do continually can put me in a place of health and safety, or fear and dysfunction. Yes, prayer and meditation are primary to establishing conscious contact with my Higher Power, in each breath; yet in every moment during my days I can choose to breathe into the presence of the cavalry, or better said, God.

WAIT . . . What Am I Thinking? Are they thoughts of love, health, protection? I continuously train my mental missionaries (thoughts) to keep me in a safe, God-centered space.

So Breathe It.

November 14
THE STILL SMALL VOICE

I must admit I've never been spoken to by an old man with a long beard looking down upon me from the clouds; nor by a man with brown hair and beard, a crown of thorns, wearing a long robe and sandals. However, I know in my heart of hearts that I've had conscious contact with both God and the Christ spirit. For that matter, I believe everybody does have and has had contact with their Creator. The question becomes one of listening and understanding to where He is communicating from.

The still small voice within is indeed God, the Christ spirit, or what you choose to call it. The essence of prayer and breathing conditioning is one of initiating conscious contact with our Higher Power. When I gently breathe during my quiet sitting times, and I have a thought of love, this is God generating love within my being. Thoughts of gratitude go both ways; both God and I share thankfulness for each other. Is not a parent grateful for its child's mere existence?

Rationalizing God's still small voice within is a sure way of breaking the connection that is the clear reception of the eternal transmission, never the source of it.

So Breathe It.

November 15
BREATHING CONDITIONING

Breathing conditioning affects every dimension of our existence. Poor breathing patterns or habits can be so deeply ingrained within us that we usually are not aware of them. Yet the effects are noticed from time to time when we realize that we are holding or limiting our breathing on a regular basis. As with Wellativity's Principle 1, declaring we need help to manage this aspect of health and wellness is the first step. The Power within you has guided you to these readings (Principle 2), which in turn will help you back to the joy of movement (breathing).

These pages are designed for daily reading. However, making notes, referring back to the book as often as you find the need, and sharing the benefits with others will all help your conditioning program. Breathe. Now slowly, breathe; now possibly smile as you inhale and close your eyes for a moment of gratitude during the exhale. You've just invested in your health, spirituality, and overall wellbeing.

To be aware is to be alive.

So Breathe It.

November 16
COLLECTIVE ENERGY

We've all had the experience of entering into a space where the type of shared energy or feeling was clear as a bell. How easy it is to find ourselves being taking away by the collective force, much like being pulled into the ocean by a strong undertow. Having been a lifeguard, I was taught that an effective way to deal with the dangerous pull of water was to swim up or down parallel to the beach, rather than to try to fight the current directly. The gist is that by changing your perception and vantage point, you can usually find a spot that's much less forceful.

When I find myself in the midst of a collective energy that I would consider negative or unhealthy, I can gain a healthy distance by acknowledging myself for being aware of it. This gives me the space to breathe, notice my thoughts, and remember I have a choice! Rather than fighting the energy directly, in each breath I gently gain the breathing room to approach the situation from a different angle.

At any moment I can choose to see things differently. This is a truth that can set me free to make a compassionate and healthy difference.

So Breathe It.

November 17
TIRED BREATHING

I recently had the opportunity to take a client to her home after a surgical procedure. Having just been under anesthesia, she was dizzy. Moreover, her movements were uncoordinated and sluggish. After she walked up the two long flights of stairs to her apartment, she stopped at the last step and almost fell backward due to feeling faint. I realized at that point that her primary breathing muscle (the diaphragm) must have been fatigued. This would explain the lack of oxygen in her blood, which could result in passing out.

For our purposes here, realizing when we are so tired that breathing may be impaired is critical. Rarely is it more important to take several full, deep, and slow breaths. Whether we're jumping up after sitting or lying down for a while, or just waking up, the cost of not letting your breathing catch up with you can be drastic. By simply initiating standing up on an exhale we can build a safeguard habit with many benefits.

It may be as simple as a deep conscious breath; which can be seen as "Making a choice to allow God's power within to help us live healthy lives" (Principle Three, becoming completely willing to have God within help you live healthy lives).

So Breathe It.

November 18
REMAINING TEACHABLE

For adults, it can be beneficial to have the appearance of confidence. I've found for myself that this trait can easily get in the way of learning, experiencing things from different perspectives, and even being OK with not knowing what we don't know. When you become aware that an unwarranted confidence is encroaching, it's wise to breathe a moment of balance and openness. It can be as simple as humbly asking our Higher Power to help us in remaining teachable.

When we get in the habit of constriction, which can often look like too much ego-based thinking, God gets eased out of the picture, that is: "Easing God Out" (EGO). When we allow this to happen we cannot remain teachable by Him. Our minds or brains are fabulous processors of information. This can be and so often is very different from receiving direct communications from our Source of Life within.

How can I see things differently in this moment? A **Course in Miracles** *says, "There is another way of looking at the world." Any question we can ask ourselves that keeps us in the newness of each moment helps to maintain open communications from the One.*

So Breathe It.

November 19
INTO THE BEYOND

I recently watched a dear friend pass into the beyond. Writing this Daily Breath with tears in my eyes, I am pressed to include all of my feelings. Although Roberta was in much pain throughout much of her life, this merciful taking by God does not remove the deep sadness the people who cared for her experienced. In my prayers I continually breathe into the sadness and the joy. The joy is in the knowing in my heart of hearts what awaits her, as well as all of us.

Thank You, God. Although we usually don't understand Your plan, thank You for the gift of being able to grow in faith during our most trying times. When we breathe Your life into our bodies, we also breathe faith into our souls. Let us all pray to remember You never forsake any of us, ever. Thank You. Amen.

So Breathe It.

November 20
COMFORT ZONE

Living in a comfort zone can be a beautiful thing. Breathing comes easier; peace is not something just to pray for, but an enjoyable experience. Once we've obtained a niche that works for us, why try anything else? My belief is that God planted the seed in us to grow and expand, just like the very universe we live in does; growth can be anything but comfortable.

The paradox with the discomfort of growing is the peace that comes with knowing we are indeed evolving. Yes, with a few full and expansive breaths we can take in the knowledge of expanding ourselves to be more loving, faithful, and God-centered in all experiences. Growth can and usually is messy, but to be a true pioneer for the betterment of humanity, we had best get comfortable with letting go of the short-term comfort zones, for long-term peace and well-being for all.

"What good is sitting alone in your room . . . life is a cabaret, old chum . . ."

So Breathe It.

November 21
THE WOUNDED HEALER

A common misconception in the healing arts is that people who serve as healing channels are healed and/or have no significant defects. In my experience, this is anything but the truth. As a matter of fact, the more damage the "healer" has endured and has firsthand reference to, the more potential he or she has toward rendering effective empathy in their service. Integrity and appropriate training are a must, but if the caregiver shows signs of being wounded, does this not add to the humanness that is so often being dropped out of all areas of services?

When I was in school being trained as a health professional, a teacher once said: "You will be surprised that when you feel your worst, a patient may tell you at the end of a session that you did your best work ever!" Having proven this statement true many times, I now breathe, pray, and meditate for God's will to work in and through me before I work, regardless of my own hurt and pain.

God, grant me the serenity to accept the things of the past,
Courage to do the next right thing; and
The wisdom to allow Thy will to be done, in each breath.
Amen.

So Breathe It.

November 22
LOVINGLY REAL

The truth, like a surgeon's scalpel, can be used to promote life or to injure. I personally, most often at the time unknowingly, have used the truth as an unsupportive tactic. In other words, I've used wisdom to defend myself, or to attack another when I was unwilling to come from a compassionate place. Apologizing, if possible, may be the next right thing to do, but in the long run, I must live, breathe, and deal with the deeper feelings that come with abusing the gift of knowledge.

I've learned to ask myself some questions with respect to when and how to use what I see as the truth: Does this need to be said by me? Does this need to be said by me now? Can the person(s) see the truth in a given situation without my injecting my version? How may I be as lovingly real with my support? Almost always there's an available moment to breathe in between each of those questions.

God, help me to help myself to remember that coming from a loving place is as valuable, if not more valuable, than the speaking of Your truth. Thank You for giving me the opportunity to share Your wisdom, while always keeping my intentions in check. Amen.

So Breathe It.

November 23
HE SAW THE NEGATIVE . . .

There has been much said about how Jesus dealt with evil and negativity. How could he have confronted vast adversity and still remained God-centered? It's also said that at times He himself battled with His own demons. No one is sure at what point He mastered being in the world but not of it. His being the son of God, a prophet, and/or the Messiah is for each person to come to terms with. However, when receiving the infinite lessons and wisdom He came here to give, is it not most important to focus on the message rather than the messenger?

Eric Butterworth taught that Christ indeed was aware of the negativity in the world, but it's not what He focused on! Every hour of every day, this is an application with all of us. What judgments, perceptions, and evaluations will we choose to focus on, or let go of, in pursuit of staying grounded in the love and power of God? One by one, we acknowledge and accept what our minds are predisposed to think; as we breathe into the truth that God's will is being done, the way is cleared for us to be His channels.

As the Zen masters refer to negative thinking: "It's as if a burning ember landed on your sleeve; the sooner you brush it off, the less damage is done.

So Breathe It.

November 24
THEY SAY

When I was a bit younger I was part of an organization that provided counseling on a group level. Every time one of us was being held accountable for our actions, we were asked, "Where did you hear that?" Invariably one of us would respond, "They say that's the way it is." At that point the counselor would instruct the one being held accountable to go around to the whole community asking: "Who is they?" Mind you, in this community one of the worst things you could do was to outwardly display anger. So you might imagine how many deep breaths were used in order to manage our affects.

What the counselor was attempting to teach was accountability and ownership of our actions. This lesson has wide-reaching validity for everyone. How often do all of us just assume things are the way they are, because we've heard people say they have heard that's the way it is. More often than not, I have found it in my best interest to not automatically settle for the way "they say" things are without some degree of questioning. During this questioning, conscious breathing can help to keep me grounded away from acting too aggressively.

When I witness injustice, misconceptions, untruths, and perpetrations in any form, I breathe as I turn my own need to be right over to my Higher Power.

So Breathe It.

November 25
YOU CAN DO IT!

It's always nice to hear someone say you can do something that you're having doubts about. The onlooker clearly sees something in you that you may not be in touch with. Changing our negative beliefs means changing our minds, which in turn will be changing how and what we think (in this case about ourselves). The more ways you come up with to interfere with a negative disposition, the better chance there is in loosening the thoughts and beliefs that may not be serving your highest good.

Books, prayers, making notes, displaying affirmations, talking to trusted support are just some of the common techniques we all can benefit from. When we see the negativity, we breathe, remember one of the positive thoughts, and most of all humbly ask God to take away the thing that does not represent who you really are.

God knows you can do it! Other people know you can do it! But there's nothing as sweet as YOU knowing you can do it!

So Breathe It.

November 26
IT CAN'T EVER BE TAKEN

It can't ever be taken, damaged, or harmed in any way. That is the spirit of God that lives within the heart and soul of all beings that he has created. When we know this, when we TRULY KNOW this, a full and joyous breath easily fills our lungs. In addition to his eternal life, our experiences and growth cannot be marred or stolen from us either. So when we tend to tense up about the transient material things in our lives, let's be reminded of the all-powerful and ever-present God that knows nothing of lack.

However, what can be taken from us is our fear, our defects of character, and all that would get in the way of conscious contact with the God of our understanding. To be meek and of childlike innocence when asking for the removal of these things is what's eluded to in almost all holy scriptures. "Please, God, take these mean and scary things away from me and the ones I love. Thank you! Amen."

If indeed Thy Will is being done on earth as it is in heaven, thank God the meek shall inherit the earth.

So Breathe It.

November 27
BEING ALTERED

With respect to "being altered," I'm referring to anything that significantly infringes on our peace, more specifically, our conscious connection with the God of our understanding. Drugs, alcohol, certain foods, and extreme emotions are obviously just a few examples of being disconnected or altered. No matter what it may be for any of us, using our breathing will always initiate a healthy step in a life-affirming direction.

Mind you, it's not the intent here to judge or condemn the inevitable conditions we will all be challenged by. As a matter of fact, for myself, some of the aforementioned have been experiences in which the hand of God has lifted me by the nape of my neck back into safety. Almost always, His intervention was preceded by my surrendering during prayer that was accompanied by, yes, conscious breathing.

God, I offer myself to Thee, to build with me and do with me as Thou wilt. Relieve me of the bondage of self, that I may better do Thy Will.

So Breathe It.

November 28
NEVER THE SAME OLD SAME OLD

Most people I know have at least one or two pet peeve phrases. Ranking as one of mine is when I greet someone and ask how they are, and they say, "Same old same old." Depending on the day (actually, on my mood), I choose among the many replies I have locked and loaded. One that takes a lot of growth on my part is a deep breath, a smile, and a nod of understanding. Being completely honest here, when my lower self responds, I use a form of truth as a righteous statement such as: "This is a brand-new moment never lived before; how can you be doing the same old thing in the same old way?"

When I find myself defaulting to judgmental responses to just the words, and not what people are really saying, I'm the one missing out on what's actually being communicated. For instance, if I'm able to breathe deep and make the effort to ground myself within, I have a shot at a charitable and compassionate understanding toward even an apparently boring statement. What the person may actually be saying is: "I'm having difficulty living in the moment and staying connected to God."

Aren't most of us challenged to live in the miracle of the here and now, or more simply put, living in the moment? You and I are more alike than not. Knowing that helps us to be more loving than judgmental. Amen.

So Breathe It.

November 29
STEPPING UP

We all have stages in our lives when God, people in our lives, and/or ourselves expect us to step up to a higher level of living. Whether we've intentionally worked toward a goal or it's just in our path, the importance in sticking with the basic skills of staying connected or In-Powered cannot be overemphasized. No matter how many of these Daily Breaths you've read, you know conscious breathing is first and foremost to any other benefits you may receive.

I've heard many times that we're either moving forward or backward but are never stationary for very long. Yes, God may be carrying us during certain times. However, the risk of failing is inherent in all forms of growth. I'm sure our true Father knows when to place us on our feet and nudge us to walk next to him as co-creators. He will not betray us, ever.

We were given a will of our own. It's my belief that in the evolution of the human spirit, the prayer will not just be "Thy Will Be Done," but more akin to "May our Wills be one. Amen."

So Breathe It.

November 30
THE CLASSROOM

If one looks at life as a learning experience, when can we truly say that we are not in a classroom of one form or another?

Hands down the finest computer ever designed is our brain, thank God! This bio-mainframe is constantly receiving, assimilating, and applying information on countless levels. What a blessing it is that we don't need to make our brain do its work.

If we venture deeper, our spiritual journey can be seen as a nonstop learning experience in the classroom called planet Earth. Just imagining how much is going on in and around us makes me take a deep breath in order to not get overwhelmed. Will you do that now?

Even the most uneducated, inexperienced, and immature human being is performing countless functions at light-speed, or should I say at God-speed. To know that beyond our perception and appearances, EVERYBODY is nothing short of a spectacular creation helps to build a universal respect for everyone we come in contact with.

So Breathe It.

December 1
THE STILL SMALL VOICE WITHIN

Being still implies a lack of movement and a type of quietness. A small voice can be understood as not loud, large, or intrusive in any way. This Daily Breath is asserting that "the still small voice within" is God's individualized and ceaseless communication in each of our souls.

The essence of Wellativity and its Daily Breath readings is helping us to use all means toward listening and responding to God within us. Breathing is our gift from God that offers us great value. It can be used to quiet our minds, increase our energy, and sustain our bodies throughout our lives. In a certain way our gentle breathing can be seen as God telling us that He not only loves us but is granting us yet more life. It's not a problem if you don't hear Him now; He's not going anywhere where you and I can't find Him.

Although the winds of heaven may dance between us, His whispers, His whistles, and His gusts speak much of the same message to you and me: "It's safe and natural to love and be loved." Shhh, can you hear that?

So Breathe It.

December 2
I AM, AND I HAVE

When I think of what I am, I see that I am a soul created by and from God. Yes, we emanate a spirit with all our unique qualities. I like to believe that my soul is made of the substance we call love, and in turn it's the essence of what all of us are made of. When I pray I do my best to get my humanness out of the way, let go, and breathe in the reality of who I truly am, with nothing added.

So often we say what we are currently feeling or having as an experience, such as being angry, rich, happy, excited, etc. The truth is, we experience all of those things at different times in our lives. It may seem as a simple difference in semantics to say "I'm having an experience" versus "I am feeling." But I find it very helpful to separate in my language what and who I am when sharing what I'm currently experiencing. It gives me the breathing space to remember who I am.

We are all made in His image, which means created out of the very fabric of His being. God is love and all that He creates originates from that love. Amen.

So Breathe It.

December 3
SMOKE

The Daily Breath is geared toward conditioning us to have healthier breathing habits. Through our days it is intended that we remember these readings in order to increase the awareness of our respiration. Making adjustments with breathing can come voluntarily or involuntarily; the source in which adjustments are needed can be positive or negative.

There are few better reminders (especially for nonsmokers) of how needed and precious our breathing is than when we take in a lungful of smoke. One of our choices in dealing with this is to condemn the origin of smoke. However, all of us know how upsetting on every level this can be. I propose to you that the next time you encounter smoke, do not stop at the need to judge it or its source, but remember that putting a positive spin on the situation, like the Daily Breath, can bring you back to a healthier way of breathing. This accomplishes two things: it diffuses our negative impulses and provides a better oxygen intake.

This too shall pass.

So Breathe It.

December 4
LIVING FOREVER

Several doctrines speak of our souls being eternal, which implies that who we are shall live forever. From a human, or ego, perspective, this can be a daunting concept. If we imagine all of our character defects challenging us endlessly, who would want to live forever? Maybe the idea of eternal life can be better understood when we grasp what living in the here and now means.

Let's breathe in as we whisper, "Be here," and breathe out, saying, "Now." Doing this several times can produce a wonderful peaceful experience, even without our understanding why or how. There are so many ways to affirm the essence of living in the moment. Like, "Live for today," "Don't worry about tomorrow, it will take care of itself," "One day at a time," etc. Whatever helps you to be in the moment is unique for you. You might consider spending some time each day, while consciously breathing, to recall what it means to you to live in the eternal moment of right now.

It is always right now, and again, right now. Each breath, each thought, and each being can really only be in the now. Our minds are what need to change; that's it; THIS IS IT!

So Breathe It.

December 5
LIFESAVER

There have been several decisive times during my lifetime when I was close to physical death. Honestly, they were also some of the most spiritual moments I've experienced. The point in sharing this is in the hope that if there is a person reading this Daily Breath who knows he or she is nearing the dying experience, or is painfully considering suicide, I can relate to both ways of being very close to going into the beyond.

Let's consciously breathe for a few moments. I don't pretend to have answers for one who is close. However, you may consider that you've already endured so much to this point, and God has certainly enabled you to survive to this moment. My prayer for you is that in these most trying moments, you reach as deep as you can and ask God to give you what's needed to survive for yet another moment of His life-giving breath. He has not abandoned you, and never will.

In Christ's most difficult moments on the cross, it is said that He cried out, "My God, my God, why have you forsaken me?" We are also shown that this was never the case. God had His plan. Can we just live on and let God's plan unfold?

So Breathe It.

December 6
RELAPSE MODE

In recovering from any addiction it's understood that one is in a "relapse mode" long before the actual fall or slip occurs. With an effective support network consistently being used, this mode of being may not be acted upon. With more subtle forms of affliction, like overindulgence, self-sabotage, and general defiance of what's best for us, there are clear cut signs (modes of behavior) that can be used to our advantage, if noticed.

If you've recently been in a less-than-healthy mode of behavior, becoming aware of every aspect of being is the first step. Consciously breathing while noticing the judgments, negative energy, and all your behaviors surrounding a potential "acting out" is your best move. A simple synopsis of Wellativity's first three principles can be a good defense when remembered.

Principle One: "surrender": admitting the power the desires are having over you; breathe.
Principle Two: "faith": acknowledging that the power of God is able to help you; breathe.
Principle Three: "choice": making a conscious choice to allow His power within to help you; breathe.

Appearances can seem bad, evil, and negative. If we take the next healthy step, these apparent conditions can make us stronger and wiser beings of the light. In making these choices, we see that being a victim of the world becomes an "unreality."

So Breathe It.

December 7
WHEREVER I GO, THERE I AM

From a self-improvement perspective, when looking at all that has happened in our lives, it could be said that whatever we've been involved with, the one constant was that we were there. When considering problems, mishaps, and apparent accidents, the first step in taking an inventory is our presence in the event. It helps me to ground myself by breathing deep when taking responsibility for the events in my life. It's not about blame, shame, or guilt but on some level my choice to be where I was.

From a spiritual vantage point, the "I am" can be seen as God and/or our Higher Power. For me, "Wherever I go, there I am" means no matter what has, is, or will happen to me, GOD IS ALWAYS PRESENT. When I breathe, saying, "I am that I am," I can't help but be comforted by the truth that my true parent is guiding and possibly carrying me through all, in all. Amen.

Christ said, "Be still and know that I am God." I believe His message was that we all are individualized expressions of the One. Just as a wave has all the components of the ocean, it can never be separated from its source. Hallelujah, so it is for us too.

So Breathe It.

December 8
GIANT STEPS

As a child I used to play a game called "Giant Steps." The goal was to get from the starting point to the leader (who was called the Mother) by asking in the appropriate manner to step closer to the Mother. "Mother, may I please take a giant step?" was the request to be graciously asked to the Mother's liking. Upon approval, our physical ability to take the biggest step or leap forward was the additional challenge to reach the finish first.

In a mental, physical, and spiritual context are we not all doing a similar process toward getting closer to the God of our understanding? In Principles 6 and 7 we prepare and humbly ask God for what we need. During prayer it helps me to first focus on my breathing, which in turn produces a calmness that I need to release the grip of my ego. Then I am downsized enough to humbly enter into the space of spiritual communion with the Almighty.

"Take your shoes off before you step on holy ground." In the scriptures, does this not mean to show respect, to become vulnerable, and to remove impediments between you and God?

So Breathe It.

December 9
IS THIS IT?

I believe all of us at one time or another have asked, "Is this all that life is for me?" When I've found myself asking that question, it's usually not from an In-Powered, grounded, or God-centered consciousness. Wellativity sees the habitual need to perceive our lives from such a negative energy as one of the crossover afflictions that can be at the root of many dangerous habits. When I'm able, I do my best to go one step further by asking, "Why am I choosing to see life from such a desolate and scarce place?"

Becoming aware of our negative thought patterns, without thinking we need to change anything, is the first step toward making healthy adjustments in our lives. Changing thoughts, energy, and consciousness (while fully breathing) is usually wise before we look outside of ourselves for fulfillment. In truth, asking "Is this it?" is our Higher Power's way of urging us to look deeper for what can be found only in the spiritual realm.

THIS IS IT! can be one of the most powerful statements toward living in the moment. In this eternal moment, we can breathe in joy, faith, hope, love, trust, excitement, peace, etc. The menu is a large one.

So Breathe It.

December 10
IN GOD'S TIME

The statement "in God's time" is filled with many implications. The first that comes to my mind is patience. Humans seem to view this "letting things happen in God's time, or being patient" as a common challenge that we face in almost every endeavor. Who hasn't needed to take several deep breaths while attempting to arrive at a destination or yearning for something to come to them?

When we gain a more spiritual perspective, "Thy Will be done," "All is in Divine order," and "Let go and let God" are all fundamental when considering "in God's time." Any of these affirmations is appropriate to be coupled with our breathing when remembered.

If we are ever in question of the exactitude of God's spatial timing, just look out into the night sky. Among the billions and billions of stars are planets that revolve around their suns with a precision just as our own. We can breathe a comforting breath as we affirm ALL is truly in Divine order. Amen.

So Breathe It.

December 11
MANTRAS

In short, a mantra is a word, phrase, and/or sound used to induce a certain state of consciousness. I was recently given a mantra by my therapist for a business trip. It was: "BUSINESS ONLY." If you knew the details of where and with whom I was to be going on this trip, I have no doubt that most everyone would have agreed it was the perfect mantra to breathe into several times an hour. Keeping the peace between all involved was the intent. For me that meant Godliness.

I notice everybody who is alive, awake, and breathing has a vibration of energy, which is in accord with their level of consciousness; the fact is, we are able to consciously change our thoughts, and this definitely impacts our effectiveness in the outer world. When we awaken in the morning it's wise to notice where our thoughts are at and see if we can reach for a higher level of consciousness.

Some may be given a mantra by a spiritual leader, which is very personal and theirs indefinitely. Whether it is given to us, or we choose a prayer/mantra each morning, we align our breathing, words, and thoughts to reinforce our bond with God.

So Breathe It.

December 12
TO THE YOUTH

Trying to fit into this busy and sometimes crazy world can make the best of us frustrated. If you're fortunate, you may have a sense of what you'll be passionate for and eventually be wise enough to go for it as a career. No doubt you will have endless opportunities to use your stress-reduction breathing skills. When you hear negative things from others about your dreams for the future, breathe; consider not allowing anyone to taint your vision, ever!

Being younger, your ability to make healthy habits is a lot easier than that of older adults who may be fixed in their ways. This is a blessing for you! There will be some things you'll try that God is telling you are not healthy or right. Do your best to use your breathing to calm your thoughts so you may hear the unending voice of wisdom. You may not always know which way to turn, but your best bet is to get good at pausing, breathing deep, and, when appropriate, closing your eyes in order to listen to your heart's desire, which is always leading you in the right direction.

It's OK not to know. In the same breath you can trust yourself completely. Being caring and compassionate is born of courage, strength, and God.

So Breathe It.

December 13
FOOD CHALLENGES

There is no doubt how challenging what we choose to eat can be. Our eating habits touch every area of our existence. From being spiritually connected, to the years we live, to emotional comfort and discomfort—we can see this challenge as a burden or as a blessing in which to demonstrate all life skills. In every situation, communication with our body, our common sense, and our Higher Power presents invaluable support.

Being aware that I'm going into, in the midst of, or finishing a "food challenge" is the first (and often overlooked) step. Then utilizing a priceless pause to breathe and to listen opens the door to healthier opportunities. Regardless of what I choose, building the consciousness or muscle of choice is the best defense toward automatically responding to habits that it would serve me best to transform.

A common thread that binds us all is our God-given ability to freely choose. Without this freedom, our evolution or growth would be limited. If we're in the middle of learning to make healthier choices, let's thank God that He still believes we can! How do we know this? Because you're still granted another choice.

So Breathe It.

December 14
PRE-WORKOUT

I have not yet met a person who doesn't experience some resistance to exercising. How each of us deals with the discussion in our minds is the crux of healthy living. In-Powering wellness through communication begins with this conversation with ourselves, then with others if needed. In consciously pausing to breathe, this enables us to listen to both sides, as nonjudgmentally as possible.

If we come into a day telling ourselves we must work out and eat well, we run the risk of not letting God work through us toward our highest good. Yes, consistency with healthy habits pays off well, but forcing or being overly willful with making positive adjustments may very well zap whatever joy there is for us in the art of choosing wisely.

There's a time and place for being firm with ourselves. Coming from a place of compassionate understanding, which is inherent to being In-Powered, can often melt even the hardest bars to what may be holding us hostage.

So Breathe It.

December 15
DRIVING

If there ever was an ideal topic for a Daily Breath, it certainly would be all that's involved with driving a car—fear, anger, impatience, excitement, concentration just for starters. It would be hard to tell you how many times my partner Laura has asked me: "Is that how Mr. Wellativity wants to be driving?" Then it would be followed by: "You might consider taking a few deep breaths!" God bless her soul.

A balance of inner and outer awareness is optimal for driving in all circumstances; breathing is not only one of our most effective tools for making healthy adjustments but is also an accurate barometer of our mental, emotional, and physical condition. Praying to and with God while behind the steering wheel is a sure bet toward a safe journey. Here's Wellativity's affirmative version of the Serenity prayer:

God, I know You've granted me the serenity to accept the things I cannot change;
The courage to change the things I can (especially my thoughts and breathing); and
The wisdom to know the difference. Amen.

So Breathe It.

December 16
HOPE

By definition, hope is the feeling that what is wanted can be had or that events will turn out for the best. When we look closer at what we are "hoping for" in our lives, the list can be extensive. However, when I ask myself what I really long for, I can count the items on one hand. The part of me or my spirit that lives more in the presence of God does not have the same aspirations as my ego does. For that matter, the more I let go of my need for better and different things of this world, the more my hope transforms into faith and trust.

Hope is a beautiful thing. It's just when we find that we are allowing it to encroach on the desire for God's will to be done in and around our lives, we would be well advised to breathe. Go within and breathe our way back to a conscious connection with the Divine.

Let go and let God; Trust the process; Thy will be done. These are the thoughts that enable us to keep faith and hope balanced.

So Breathe It.

December 17
MR. WELLATIVITY

"Is that the way Mr. Wellativity should act?" Usually I've been asked that when I'm doing something that doesn't meet a person's expectations of how an enlightened or God-centered individual should behave. I might say, "I'm not a prophet, saint, or a spiritual leader." Wellativity's message is one of improving communications toward wellness. Let this stand for the record and hopefully for anyone on the path of healing or self-improvement: Growth can be messy; the goal is progress not perfection. Let's be responsible for cleaning up our messes as soon as possible.

In my opinion, the universal barometer of growth is the point at which we notice the need for a healthy adjustment and the time in which we expedite it as nonjudgmentally as possible (Principle 10). Hopefully this is accompanied by full, unforced, conscious breathing, along with whatever prayer, affirmation, and restorative action that would work best in a given situation.

Forgiveness is the key to happiness. God's level of forgiveness, if it's ever really needed, is unknown to us. However, as we forgive ourselves and others, our lines of communication become less encumbered with static.

So Breathe It.

December 18
EDUCATING CHILDREN

Whether we are parents raising children or not, the fact is that all of us are educating children. They watch how we deal with life as well as with our personal challenges. Living by example, Wellativity's 12th Principle, does not just include what is seen. If we are hiding unhealthy behaviors from the sight of the children, this can ultimately end up being detrimental. The truth is, children also learn by the energies that surround them. So if we choose to hide, sneak, and/or lie on behalf of only what they see, on a certain level they know. This speaks to the essence of truly training our young ones physically, emotionally, and spiritually.

In my opinion, communicating our own personal challenges in an appropriate, safe, and honest way will teach children that what we do may not be healthy and not OK for them, but that we are working at making healthier adjustments. What an opportunity this can be to demonstrate many of Wellativity's principles to the ones who are so impressionable.

You may consider meditating (breathing) and praying about these situations before you go one step further and also consult your trusted support network.

God, please help me to help myself so I may better serve the children of this world, who are in desperate need of healthy teachers, guides, and parents. Amen.

So Breathe It.

December 19
WHAT GOD IS

We've all heard so many humans professing to know what and who God is. Being completely honest, does any of us really know the answer? Let's compare this understanding to our oceans. Most of us have seen as well as been in the ocean. We know characteristics and elements of its make-up, but even the marine biologist will say we know more about outer space than we do of our own oceans. The point here is the bit we think we know about God is extremely limited at best.

Common sense, logic, and personal experience can go miles past all the books and sermons with regard to an individual understanding of who and what our Creator is to only me; it may be totally different to you. It's my belief that God lives and breathes in me. He not only created breathing but helps to remind me of its many benefits. When I'm reminded to take a deep breath, I see that as God's direct communication to me, through whomever or whatever form He uses. Thank You, God, for the many endless messages You give me every day of my life. Amen.

Allowing God to be God, in and through us, has unlimited potential. Believing in, preaching about, swearing to, fighting wars over Him is our individual choice. However, thinking we understand Him may only be a consolation prize. Let's do our best to accept God just as He/She/It is. It's been said that we were made in His image, not the other way around.

So Breathe It.

December 20
I WISH FOR YOU

I am uncomfortable telling people what kind of a day to have or how to be when saying goodbye. I know that saying "have a good day" means well, but my understanding of the kind of day their Higher Power needs them to have may not necessarily be qualified as "good" or "pleasant." I realize this can be seen as simple semantics, but a lot of phrases such as these have become mainstream orders that may not fit the spiritually orientated person.

If I take a moment or two to breathe and be with how I'd like to part from a person, it often entails a wish or a prayer. This is a spacious, spiritual way of offering my energy for them to receive or not. "I'm praying for your safety and happiness." Or, "I wish you all the healing and well-being that you want." To me this shows someone that our parting has some kind of authenticity rendered on my part. You might consider breathing into a few thoughts of what is just accepted routine. You might not only add some extra meaning for the one you are with, but you could very well offer a healthy shift in energy.

The question is not so much as to the words used but rather the presence, the compassion, and the authenticity put forth.

So Breathe It.

December 21
NOTHING BORING ABOUT IT

Being a personal trainer for decades, I've found it's no secret how most people feel about exercising or working out. "I hate it; it's boring; I only do it not to be fat" are some of the statements I'm confronted with on a regular basis. It would be easy to put the blame and fault on individuals as a reason why so many of us have acquired unhealthy perceptions toward fitness, but let's focus on where to go from here.

If there were a supreme antidote to our negative disposition toward exercising, it would have to be GRATITUDE. I personally never appreciated my ability to walk about unassisted until I was disabled for years with a leg brace as a boy. Not only myself but many have professed this truth: "We don't appreciate what we have until it's gone." The next time you work out, or are thinking about it, breathe, and consider this: exercising is investing toward a lifetime of mobility; it also is reducing the risk of many diseases; it is a special way to thank the One who gave you the ability to choose to work with Him toward a healthier existence.

Thank You, God, for all that I have and do not have. Let my efforts toward taking better care of my health and fitness show my gratitude.

So Breathe It.

December 22
ZEN PASSENGER

Being the passenger in a car can be stressful for many reasons. If the stress comes from how the driving is being done, saying something may be necessary. However, once the communication of concern is put forth, the passenger's best bet toward safety is remaining grounded in a spiritual place within. In these trying moments remember that prayer works! Using Wellativity's Principle 3 (and step 3 in the 12-step program), it's about turning over our concerns to God/our Higher Power. Taking a deep breath, we ask God to work through the driver toward a safe trip.

God knows who's in the car and what is best for all involved. The question for ourselves is: "Do we trust that all is in Divine order, or are we worrying if God can indeed take care of everyone's safety?" Let's not underestimate the impact of our energies while we maintain a prayerful, or Zen passenger, state of being.

In the practice of Zen it is often suggested to just be, or do the task at hand with nothing added. It's just you and the spirit chopping the wood, or walking with a pail of water, or just being safely driven in a car to a destination.

So Breathe It.

December 23
JUDGMENTS

In our civilization there exists a wide range of what is right, wrong, good, and bad. This Daily Breath is dealing with the judgments in our minds. Let's do our best to notice how we may be letting our judgments of ourselves and others influence our perception of the way things are. Speaking for myself, when I am being judgmental of what I've done or haven't done, it often gets in my way. I believe the judgments block me from healing, from taking the next healthy action, and, most of all, hearing the communications from my Higher Power.

God loves us, NO MATTER WHAT! We've all heard millions of ways God judges us, may or may not forgive our sins, and the many other different ways God sees us. Morals and values of peace and compassion are what's needed in our world. When I become overly critical and judgmental, I do my best to breathe and remember that if I'm focused on criticism, my conscious connection with God is sacrificed.

Do we really believe all is in Divine order, or are we attempting to establish our perception of it? Being charitable with our thinking may include a whole lot of forgiveness. It's been said that forgiveness is the key to happiness.

So Breathe It.

December 24
PORTAL OF PROSPERITY

If we look at the life that's been given us as a form of prosperity, we are indeed prospering from the very start. By definition, prosperity is "a successful, flourishing, or thriving condition." To come from a place of prosperity, consciousness is a priceless skill. We could write volumes on why we so often live in a state of scarcity, but for now let's understand that we have a choice to come from abundance. Trying to convince ourselves that we have abundant finances might not be the best place to start.

Taking small and easy steps (like beginning an exercise program) is wise. Here's a Wellativity Daily Breath sample exercise: "In each breath I take, I feel the prospering effects of an abundance of oxygen all around me. Thank You, God. I breathe in again, as I acknowledge my health as a source of prosperity; breathing once more, I realize the origins of my prospering ways are linked to my infinite creativity. Thank You again, God, for the unending stream of ideas that help me to flourish. Amen."

Coming from the right direction, the lightest of winds can raise a kite to higher and higher levels. To allow the winds of your consciousness to carry you, you must start from where you are, not from where you want to be.

So Breathe It.

December 25
INTERSECTIONS

When I'm at a red light, whether on foot or in a car, I do my best to remember to really stop and reset everything from my thoughts to my breathing. This includes covering myself, the people near me, and the vehicle(s) with the light of safety. This also may include a thought of forgiveness for possible less-than-loving actions of myself and others (Wellativity's Principle 10).

During these invaluable few moments of being at an intersection, conscious breathing plays its most critical role. The meeting of two or more roads may also occur in our journeys in life. Being in the midst of countless endings and beginnings, how we approach these transitions can make all the difference between a peaceful or stressful experience. Tilling the fertile soil of our minds toward trust and faith most certainly will enable us to reap its benefits.

Every breath entails a stopping and a starting. Breathe again and again into the thought: "I let go, and let God." Let's build the habit of conscious inclusion of the light of protection and safety in all our travels.

So Breathe It.

December 26
MOBILITY

Having been disabled with a leg brace as a boy, and having worked with seniors for more than 3 decades, I know firsthand how high "mobility" ranks with regard to our health. Not having it, and with the need of assistance just to stand up, let alone walk, makes everything else seem trivial. I'm telling you this because one of the things that helps me so often to breathe easier and deeper is my ability to stand and walk with no effort or help. This is a blessing that comes from experiencing what I once did and now do not.

This topic weaves right into the value of gratitude. Think for a moment of all the things you'll be doing today. Legs, cars, buses, trains, walkers, canes, navigation systems, money, all work in tandem with our mobility. Our list of gratitude can be filled with hundreds of examples. So when we notice our breathing is cut short due to the trivial, let's all take a moment to thank God for what we have and do not have.

How can we not breathe easier after appreciating our ability to move about in our lives? Thank You, God, for all that contributes to my mobility. Amen.

So Breathe It.

December 27
DISABILITIES

Unless we are fully "able" in all areas, it is valid to say that each of us is disabled to a certain extent. It can be quite rattling to realize how many disabilities everyone has. In my life, every disability that I've been challenged by has presented infinite possibilities for growth and service. Whether it's afflictions, physical impairments, or mental shortcomings, we can breathe much easier knowing we are not alone. Judging ourselves and others for the degree of difficulties/opportunities we each have will lead to a disability toward restricting the healing flow of love and acceptance.

It can be so easy to blame others (including God) for our own shortcomings. The first step in overcoming this is to take ownership of what we can do or let go of, right here; right now. It is impossible to be looking at the past while moving forward. Try to have a few breaths while asking yourself, "What are the possibilities if I were to let go of the apparent negatives?"

It seems to be the ultimate spiritual challenge for each of us to see our cups as either half full, or half empty.

So Breathe It.

December 28
HYPNOSIS

As defined in the dictionary, hypnosis is "an artificially induced trance state resembling sleep, characterized by heightened susceptibility to suggestion." I had to smile after I read that definition. My thought was, "That's just how so many of us walk around in life!"—bombarded by advertisements, tired from stress, and looking for good feelings (mainly outside of ourselves). This is mentioned to cover the potential danger in being hypnotized or living in a hypnotic state.

On the other hand, reading *Wellativity's Daily Breath* can be a valuable conditioning or hypnotic process. I'm honestly saying, "Yes, I'd love to see you hypnotized toward remembering to breathe better all day long!" There's no way to avoid all the unhealthy suggestive influences and still be in our society. But reading The Daily Breath on a regular basis is a powerful and healthy way to help balance our hypnotic ways.

Let signals to breathe fuller become automatic, even during sleep! Write about it, speak about it, think about it, read about it; I promise that your body will be healthier for it! BREATHE HERE AND NOW!

So Breathe It.

December 29
TECHNOLOGY VS. HUMANITY

What a blessing technology can be. Without it you wouldn't be reading this Daily Breath. However, it's my belief that many of us are forgetting the most advanced machinery ever created, that being the human race, not to mention the miracle of compassionate interactions available throughout humanity. Are our devices impairing face-to-face ethics, morals, and values?

When I notice that my computerized involvement is taking up an inordinate amount of time, I do my best to stop, breathe, and say or do something nice WITH someone. "Hello, I care about you"; "Are you OK?"; "Can I help?"; "I apologize"; "Your being here helps me to feel good"—these are just some of the communications that can support us in reconnecting with our positive humanness. Moreover, putting the gadgets down, closing our eyes, and consciously breathing as we say hello, thank you, and I love You to the God within can In-Power us 10 times over.

Balance is key. Notice a sunset, hug someone, touch the Earth, stretch, smell something pleasant (breathing bonus), acknowledge a feeling, thank God for something nice—these are just a few of the ways to reconnect with humanity. What are some for you?

So Breathe It.

December 30
WELLATIVITY'S DAILY BREATH PRAYER

Wellativity acknowledges Divine Order throughout the Earth.

In every breath, of every living being, God lives.

Mean-spiritedness and evil are but guides to become more loving.

In truth, love is within all, even when it doesn't look as though it is.

Fear has no power. Love is the only Power in the universe.

Forgiveness is the key to our happiness.

I connect with God, all people, and the Earth when I consciously breathe.

In this very breath, I encircle our planet with healing light and love.

Peace, Joy, and Love are established now and forevermore. Amen.

So Breathe It.

December 31
PICK ONE

Consciousness-raising seems to be what we as individuals and as a global community are involved with more than ever. With regard to health and well-being, living in the present moment offers great payoffs. This is not such an easy task for us when all of the distractions of the world beckon for our attention. This being said, choosing or picking something(s) that helps us to return our awareness to the here and now is very wise.

To "pick one" means to choose something simple that is seen or heard in the outside world. You decide that when you become aware of your item, it's a sign to come back to where you are in the moment. I've used letters, numbers, colors, and words. The letter "G" on Tuesday may remind me to acknowledge God. On Friday the color blue could bring me back to consciously breathing. Possibly for the week the number 3 helps me to choose to come from love rather than fear. Pick one and watch what happens.

Our minds can be used to help us grow, or not. The options are endless. Yet, it will always come down to one thing: choice.

So Breathe It.

Scott Morofsky grew up and resides in New York. In addition to his battles with and overcoming of his own physical disability as a young boy and his personal involvement in recovery, he has national certification as a personal trainer by the American Council on Exercise and various other certifications in the health and fitness field. He is a New York State licensed massage therapist and a graduate of the Swedish Institute of Massage and Allied Health Sciences. As a professional, Scott has maintained a thirty-two-year private practice specializing in joint replacement rehabilitation and physical training for seniors, as well as fitness training and massage therapy, and has given lectures and taught seminars on these subjects. Spirituality has always been at the core of his work.

Made in the USA
Middletown, DE
23 June 2015